PARTNERS AND RIVALS

The Uneasy Future of China's Relationship
with the United States

PARTNERS AND RIVALS

The Uneasy Future of China's Relationship with the United States

WENDY DOBSON

UNIVERSITY OF TORONTO PRESS
Toronto Buffalo London

ISBN 978-1-4426-4752-7

∞

Printed on acid-free, 100% post-consumer recycled paper with
vegetable-based inks

Library and Archives Canada Cataloguing in Publication

Dobson, Wendy, author
Partners and rivals : the uneasy future of China's relationship with the
United States / Wendy Dobson.

Includes bibliographical references and index.
ISBN 978-1-4426-4752-7 (bound)

1. United States – Relations – China.   2. China – Relations – United
States.   3. United States – Economic conditions – 2001–.   4. China –
Economic conditions – 2000–.   I. Title.

E183.8.C5D62 2013   327.73051   C2013-905072-8

University of Toronto Press acknowledges the financial assistance to its
publishing program of the Canada Council for the Arts and the Ontario
Arts Council.

Canada Council   Conseil des Arts
for the Arts   du Canada

ONTARIO ARTS COUNCIL
CONSEIL DES ARTS DE L'ONTARIO
50 YEARS OF ONTARIO GOVERNMENT SUPPORT OF THE ARTS
50 ANS DE SOUTIEN DU GOUVERNEMENT DE L'ONTARIO AUX ARTS

University of Toronto Press acknowledges the financial support of the
Government of Canada through the Canada Book Fund for its publishing
activities.

Contents

List of Tables and Figures   vii

Introduction   3

1 The Changing Shape of the World Economy   17

2 China's Incomplete Transformation, or What It Means to Age before Becoming Rich   34

3 Turning Point or Countdown to Crisis?   47

4 China's Growing International Footprint   73

5 Twenty-First-Century Rivalry? Chinese and US Views of Each Other   90

6 China and Global Governance   103

7 The Inside Game   120

8 The Outside Game   134

9 Partners and Rivals: The Uneasy Relationship   147

Notes   151

Bibliography   167

Acknowledgments   179

Index   183

Tables and Figures

Tables

1.1 Comparisons of Gross Domestic Product: China, Japan, Germany, and United States, 2000 and 2010   18
1.2 Comparative Indicators: China, Japan, Germany, and United States   20
1.3 China as a Major Trading Partner, 2011   30
1.4 China's Foreign-Exchange Reserves, 2005–12   31
6.1 China in Global Governance   108

Figures

1.1 The Comparative Growth of the United States, China, Japan, and German, 1970–2010   22
1.2 China's Holdings of US Treasury Bonds, 2001–13   31
2.1 China's Dependency Ratio and Population Growth, 1950–2100   35
2.2 China's Productivity Performance in International Perspective, 1990 and 2010   38
2.3 China's Urban Population, 1953–2012   41
4.1 Exports and Imports, China and United States, as Shares of Global Trade, 2000–1   75
4.2 Outward Stocks of Direct Foreign Investment: China, Hong Kong, Japan, and United States, 2000–11   76
6.1 Changing Shares of Global Output, 2005–30   104
8.1 Asia's Trade "Tracks"   139

PARTNERS AND RIVALS

The Uneasy Future of China's Relationship with the United States

Introduction

Competition between the United States and China is inevitable but conflict is not. This is not the Cold War ... China is acting purely in its own national interests. It is not interested in changing the world.

– Lee Kuan Yew[1]

As they strolled together in the morning sunlight at Sunnylands, California, accompanied only by their interpreters, Presidents Barack Obama and Xi Jinping, by the style and substance of their informal meeting, began to change the arc of history.

The relationship between China and the United States is central to any strategic view of the world of the twenty-first century. These two nations, the largest economies in the world, are deeply intertwined through mutual flows of goods, services, capital, and people. Their military budgets are also the largest in the world. Indeed, many predict a Great Power rivalry between them that only one can win. Their relationship in the post-war period has been a complex one, with close cooperation following President Richard Nixon's informal meetings with Mao Zedong in 1972, when both countries faced a common perceived Soviet threat. Since China's reform and opening in 1978, that relationship has waxed and waned but has become increasingly uneasy in recent years. In 2013, as Obama began his second term and Xi his ten-year mandate, the US and Chinese leaders signalled their intention to pursue a more cooperative path and invest in deeper mutual understanding, even as tensions and rivalry between their two nations continued in the Asia-Pacific region and over cyber security.

Why is there rivalry between the two? One is an established world power and the other a rising one, and the two have deeply different living standards, histories, goals, values, and institutions. History is marked by conflicts between such powers because of competition, misunderstandings, or miscalculation. Since its founding nearly two and a half centuries ago, the United States has grown from a collection of colonies into a world superpower. Over the same period China's ancient dynastic system of emperor rule declined and then collapsed, and the country suffered humiliating invasions and oppression by foreign powers; in response, following the founding of the People's Republic in 1949, Mao Zedong turned China away from the Western world for decades.

Importantly, both countries consider themselves exceptional. Americans see their democratic system as superior to all others, and their national interests as best served by spreading the virtues of democracy, market capitalism, and globalization and by maintaining order with the world's most powerful military. Chinese exceptionalism is rooted in the country's millennia-old civilization and its view of itself as the Middle Kingdom. With persistence and patience China is regaining its status as a Great Power deserving of the world's respect. Paradoxically, however, traditionally inward-looking and agrarian China, with its still-fresh memory of vulnerability and humiliation, is extraordinarily sensitive towards outsiders who are seen as offending the intense Chinese national pride in its accomplishments.

Chinese foreign policy is driven, first and foremost, by the country's domestic interests and by the Communist Party's need to legitimize its autocratic rule. China's enterprises are expanding their global footprints, and it is intent on developing the military capabilities associated with a Great Power. Yet since the Group-of-Twenty leaders' forum was created in 2008 in large part to include China, it has become apparent that China will participate but not lead. The reasons are not hard to find. First, its leaders are unwilling to take on any international obligations that might undermine the domestic goals of stability, growth, and jobs. Second, many

Chinese still see themselves as poor: from my own experiences
. in lectures and discussions in China in recent years, I have found
a broad consensus among Chinese that, although China soon
might become the world's largest economy, "we are still poor, with
many domestic problems which we must address before we can
help others."

This paradox between China's exceptionalism and its inward-
looking vulnerability was evident during high-profile broadcasts
by China Central Television (CCTV) from Beijing's Tiananmen
Square during the once-in-a-decade leadership transition in November 2012. Interviewers plied both Chinese and foreign guests
with such questions as "What is the future of China's relationship
with the United States? Is China a threat? What is China's international role?" What kind of superpower will China be?

To many westerners China is autocratic, opaque, and foreign,
with little to teach others. To many Chinese, although a rising
power has much to learn from Western powers, particularly the
United States, the lessons must be adapted to the Chinese way of
doing things and to finding the Chinese way in the world. China's
sense of vulnerability, however, remains close to the surface. Turn
on CCTV at any time of the night or day, and you will see historical battle dramas with foreigners, frequently Japanese, featured
on at least one channel. Members of the security and intelligence
communities frequently express the conviction that the United
States aims to contain China's rise in Cold War fashion, despite
the two giants' interdependence through huge flows of trade, investment, capital, and people. Such sensibilities are reflected in
Chinese leaders' goals of stability and security: to protect China's
sovereignty and territorial integrity and to build a strong economy
and nation.

All of these factors are at play in assessing the future US-Chinese
relationship. This book focuses on two main questions. First, what
does China want? Second, how can the two countries deepen the
mutual understanding and trust necessary to build a long-term,
cooperative relationship? My thesis is that the relationship can
avoid traditional Great Power competition. The Sunnyland meeting between Obama and Xi was long on style and bonhomie but

short on the substantive need to address bilateral, regional, and global issues. Its significance, however, lies in the new tone the leaders set at the top, which will influence subsequent meetings of the two countries' officials. More substance and more dialogue are needed to respect each other's goals and strategies. In a deeply interconnected world the consequences of conflict as a result of misunderstanding, miscalculation, or accident are prohibitively high, and there is little place for zero-sum politics.

Three main factors are driving this mutual need for cooperation: the depth of economic interdependence that links their fates, the major domestic challenges both countries face, and the existence of multiple channels through which to build confidence. As I argue in the early chapters, China's leaders face huge domestic challenges following more than three decades of rapid growth. The current economic model has become unsustainable and must change if China is to avoid falling into the trap of stagnant growth that ensnares many middle-income countries – and it must do this in the face of resistance on the part of powerful interests that have been the beneficiaries of the fast-growth model.

China's leaders need a stable international environment if the country is to continue to rise. To that end the relationship with the United States is key, not just as an economic partner but, significantly, as a strategic partner in Asia, where recent rebalancing of US interests has heightened China's sense of vulnerability, evoking fears of Cold War–like containment and prompting President Xi's push for a "new type of great power relations." In the second part of the book I examine what such a partnership might look like, beginning with how each country views the other, why the bilateral relationship is at an important crossroads, and what to look for in a successful resolution of differences over the next decade and beyond.

DEEP INTERDEPENDENCE

It has become commonplace to characterize Chinese-US interdependence in terms of China as the United States' "banker," but the reality is more complicated, as I show in Chapter 1. China's three-decades-long growth sprint has dominated the shift of world economic gravity to Asia, and the speed and magnitude of its re-emergence has surprised both its own leaders and the rest of the world. Another factor in the shift, however, is the change in relative growth rates of the major economic powers since the 2008 global financial crisis. Growth slowed in the United States and the European Union as both economies suffered their most serious setback since the Great Depression. The EU faces a future of continuing slow growth, to cope with which it must make difficult internal adjustments. In the United States, in contrast, the picture is brightening. Self-sustaining economic growth is resuming, despite the continued inability of Congress and the Obama Administration to agree on how to put the country's fiscal policy on a sustainable track. As well, US employment numbers are improving, spending on research and development continues to be robust, and technological breakthroughs allowing the exploitation of the country's huge deposits of shale gas and oil are reducing energy prices and improving energy security. At the subnational level, state governments are finding innovative ways to fund replacements for aging infrastructure and improve educational access and quality.[2]

For its part, China continued to sail along, spurred by generous government stimulus spending augmented by a surge in bank lending. Even as the growth model changes and China navigates through major structural changes, it will continue to depend on foreign demand for its products. A major source of that growth in the next few years is likely to be the United States.

CHINA'S DOMESTIC CHALLENGES

Among China's many domestic challenges, one that has caught the world's attention, as I discuss in Chapter 2, is its aging population even as so many people remain relatively poor. Little can be done about changing the shape of China's demographic structure, beyond supporting the rising numbers of dependents, but much can be done to increase productivity through urbanization, to invest in a higher-skilled and more creative workforce, and to make better use of existing labour by reforming the *hukou* household registration system, which restricts the rights of migrant workers.

In Chapter 3 I assess China's larger set of economic challenges. Its long-term growth prospects are quite positive if it succeeds in increasing productivity and efficiency, but, as former premier Wen Jiabao emphasized on the margins of the National People's Congress in March 2007, the current economic growth model is "unsustainable, uncoordinated, unbalanced, and unstable." Increasingly, the key question is whether China can bring about the productivity gains necessary to move from its reliance on high rates of investment onto a path of sustained growth sufficient to raise per capita incomes to Western levels.[3] To answer such a question, economists use a growth-accounting framework, analysing supply-side changes in inputs of labour, capital, land, and natural resources, and the efficiency with which they are used in production. In the early stages of industrialization, governments typically mobilize these inputs in an effort to catch up to higher-income nations. Rural populations migrate to more productive jobs in urban industry, household and corporate savings are channelled into productive investments, and changes in land use and the extraction of natural resources convert both types of savings to more productive uses. Eventually, however, the gains from mobilization dissipate – there are diminishing returns from adding another unit of capital to the existing labour force, for example – and economic stagnation looms.

Moving beyond mobilization to a new stage of development requires changes in policies and institutions – what Nobel laureate Douglass North called the "software of growth" – to change an economy's long-term growth trajectory, one that encourages economic agents to find new, more innovative ways to organize production, thereby raising productivity and getting more output from existing inputs. The software includes incentive structures that encourage workers to be more productive – by rewarding education and skills training and facilitating geographic mobility – and producers to be competitive and innovative; financial institutions that allocate capital efficiently and reward savers; legal institutions that protect property rights; and economic institutions that encourage openness to trade and finance.[4]

China, however, has made little progress since Wen's remarks, as we will see in Chapter 3 – indeed the momentum for these difficult economic reforms has since slowed. But his observation reflects a shift of attention to the distorted structure of domestic demand resulting from the growth sprint. Income inequality is growing, environmental degradation is feeding popular dissatisfaction, most of the benefits of growth have accrued to the coastal regions, leaving other regions of the country behind, and the share of China's gross domestic product (GDP) accounted for by consumption has declined as investment and net exports have driven aggregate demand.[5] Investment has been financed by the high savings rates of households, enterprises, and government, which have been mobilized and channelled into investment projects.[6] And because the savings rate has been even higher than the investment rate, China has been able to run a trade surplus.[7]

Since 2007 China has increased public spending on social programs in an effort to tackle income inequality, but the Communist Party has continued to rely on mobilizing inputs to maintain the fast growth of output and jobs it needs to maintain its legitimacy. It has taken little action to reform policies and institutions that favour producers over households and goods production over services. Income has been extracted from households and transferred to enterprises at cheap input prices. Environmental regulations have not been enforced. Sectors reserved for state-owned enterprises (SOEs) actually have expanded, restraining competition. The undervalued exchange rate has contributed to external imbalances and international tensions.

These growth-at-any-cost policies have created entrenched interest groups resistant to changes that fail to serve their interests. The paradox is that, at the same time, China's growing and increasingly vocal urban middle classes are now expecting change. China's new leaders are now having to decide whether and how to take on these vested interests. They are also motivated to seek a more stable and predictable relationship with the United States and to normalize China's participation in the global economic order.

Is China, then, its own worst enemy? The longer the delay in changing its trajectory the larger will become the economic distortions and the greater the political difficulty of correcting them. Can China's outdated policies and institutions be changed without precipitating a crisis? Do China's political masters have the vision and power to implement reforms that sustain the momentum of growth? Deng Xiaoping's famous unofficial southern tour in 1992 highlighted the need for new efforts to implement reforms, but their slowing after his retirement emphasizes the importance of such questions.[8] The individual initiative and risk taking necessary to sustain growth typically calls for less state control to encourage market forces and competition. Since returns to innovation are realized only in the future, what is needed are greater transparency, sound accounting rules, and the recognition and enforcement of rights to property, including intellectual property, no matter who the producers are or whom they know.

Much of the needed economic change probably can be accomplished with good management and determined leadership, but significant institutions also need restructuring. Corruption is endemic, but the issue is a complex one because of the autocratic role of the Party and its relationship to the legal system. Party members are widely seen to use their control and privilege to help themselves to the opportunities and winnings of economic growth while convincing themselves that the associated growth in jobs and household incomes confers on them the legitimacy to retain power. As the number of Internet users reaches half a billion and an estimated 300 million access social media, major economic disparities are now on public display. Many Chinese readily admit that their material circumstances and economic freedom have improved more in their lifetimes than they could have imagined possible. They do not object to people becoming rich from their own efforts and ingenuity – and many have done just that – but it is *how* they become rich. Many engage in rent-seeking behaviour in which privilege, connections, and corrupt practices are used to reinterpret or circumvent rules that apply to everyone else. Some observers argue that China, in fact, is two parallel states: a Party state and a legal state that applies to everyone else and that permits sometimes-brutal repression of protestors and critics by the public security apparatus.

Meanwhile the Party sincerely believes its grip on political power has been essential to China's economic success, and Party members insist that loosening its political grip risks a "Gorbachev moment," the sort of chaos into which Russia fell following political and economic liberalization in the late 1980s. The population tolerates the Party's authoritarianism because of the jobs it has been seen to have created, the rise in living standards, and increased economic freedom. On the other hand, increasing resistance from netizens, journalists, academics, and ordinary citizens implies that the Party's autocratic ways could become the source of future political and social conflict.

China's new leaders have sent mixed signals about the reform road map they intend to follow. The more cautious among them argue that rebuilding the social safety net and stepping up the pace of income redistribution are where to begin because such measures would be popular and within the central government's direct spending powers. Vastly more difficult are institutional questions about the role of the state, checks and balances on power, greater transparency, and the rule of law. In November 2012 both then-President Hu Jintao and his successor Xi Jinping emphasized their determination to tackle corruption, which is like a dark parallel reality where positions in government, SOEs, and even the military can be bought and sold and where gaming the system for personal gain occurs at all levels. Xi's public calls for the Party to respond with disciplinary action against members who consider themselves above the law are, however, only a start, and a far cry from the "newspaper test" that is applied to the behaviour of public officials in countries with a free press and an independent judiciary.

Closely related are the opacity of the relationships among those in power and how the state functions. Senior leaders have spent their lives cultivating relationships within the Party hierarchy and its systems of patronage; when they are promoted their entire staffs move with them. Advancement, although determined largely by merit, is approved by the Party's little-known Central Organization Department. Along the way, approved leaders have run huge state-owned banks or other enterprises and provinces and are highly experienced and tested. Xi Jinping, for example, was governor of two coastal provinces – Fujian with 35 million people and Zhejiang with 47 million – with per capita incomes above the national average. As they rise up the ladder these figures build networks of relationships with other powerful players and with their staffs, whose continued loyalty can be essential to their success. In return they must promote the interests of those in their networks.

Such relationships have deep historical roots in China's system of *guanxi* – informal networks of mutual trust in which personal or clan relationships or geographic proximity substitute for the rule of law. Increasingly, however, they contribute to the ambiguity of China's partly developed legal system. Successful networks built upon strong relationships of mutual trust might tolerate, even promote, the accrual of personal wealth, but, in the absence of well-defined property rights, everyone is vulnerable to score settling. If one's first allegiance is to one's family or network, is it wrong to engage in bribery or to exercise privilege in a discrete way to secure the family's or network's future? What place do the interests of broader society have in such a system?

Such dilemmas will not be resolved easily. It is common for outsiders to assume that the liberalizers will prevail and that China will become more "like us" – more democratic, more market driven, with the development of checks and balances on political power and the primacy of the rule of law. Implicit in such an assumption – that these are the attributes of an ideal system of governance – overlooks, however, the increasing confidence of Chinese elites that China will find its own way, as it always has, by comparing its historical institutions with those of other countries and adopting "Chinese characteristics."

China has always been conservative, autocratic, and hierarchical, in the Confucian tradition. The emperor ruled with a mandate from heaven that could be revoked by the people if they considered they were not wisely and justly governed. In a radical break with tradition, Mao Zedong introduced Marxist-Leninist class struggle, ostensibly to promote greater equality, by pitting the proletariat against intellectuals and the establishment. He abolished traditional institutions such as landlords and merchants and nationalized land and financial institutions. Yet even he, in assuming an emperor-like role, eventually was overtaken by historical inertia as he substituted Party cadres for Confucian scholars and bureaucrats chosen on merit. The Party continues to harness the merchant class by relying on SOEs, just as it harnesses technological change like the Internet to its own purposes. It is finding, however, the growing diffusion of interconnectedness in commercial relations, universal education, mass communication, and the growth of civil society more difficult to control, adding urgency to question of whether and how the Party will change course.

China's economic and political institutions and foreign policy are the subjects of intense domestic debates, with voices joining in along the spectrum from traditional to liberal, nationalist to internationalist. What seems likely to occur is incremental reform within the existing political system, perhaps with a consultative form of democracy and a narrower definition of individual rights, rather than the "Western-style" multiparty form, which is considered confrontational. Greater transparency gradually could reduce the regulatory thicket and increase the disclosure of personal assets by lower-level officials, while more accountability could lead to greater tolerance of efforts by citizens and civil society to monitor local governance.

Whatever directions China takes, they will be distinctively Chinese. Moreover, they will be set within the next decade. Hu Jintao's slogan was "scientific development;" Xi Jinping's is the "Chinese dream," and it could herald a new chapter in this huge and vital country's move towards reform and openness. After his first six months in office, the effect of Xi's pronouncement has been uplifting, but the concept is sufficiently vague that it has become a vessel into which people pour both their hopes and their cynicism. Some see it as an invitation to nationalists, others a vision of a strong, civilized, harmonious, and egalitarian nation, while still others deride it as too vague for parents who wish to buy safe baby formula and city dwellers who wish to breathe clean air.

Tackling China's many domestic challenges will be difficult, and progress will be measured not in months but in decades. Expectations have been raised, but managing them could absorb most of the leaders' political capital, leaving little time and attention to guide China's role in the world – particularly its relationship with the United States.

A NEW WAY FORWARD IN THE WORLD?

China's stirring is making waves beyond its borders, as I discuss in Chapter 4, and raising external expectations and questions about its future intentions and global role. Many such questions have been prompted by China's assertive behaviour since 2008 in pushing its boundary claims in offshore waters. Yet its uncoordinated economic and military activities and political bullying have served only to alarm neighbours and unravel years of efforts to conduct friendly diplomacy. In response worried neighbours have implored the United States to step up the pace of its re-engagement in the region, which, in turn, has raised Chinese sensitivities and frustrations. At the same time some of China's international footprints are more benign, even beneficial, in nature, including increasing tourism, flows of trade and investment, and the growing regional use of its currency. China's unique institutions are shaping these footprints.

How will China's relationship with the United States evolve in the Asia-Pacific region, which is central to China view of its role in the world? In Chapter 5 I look at how each views the other and itself. China's humiliation narrative influences the thinking of strategists who insist that, in refocusing on the Asia-Pacific, the United States is engaging in Cold War containment, rather than responding rationally to the region's economic dynamism. Specialists on both sides agree that China's ambivalence contrasts with the more positive attitudes of US leadership. Even so the United States could provide more strategic reassurance, both could seek ways to frame mutually acceptable goals, and both could make more use of multilateral forums where other countries can buffer bilateral frictions.

In Chapter 6 I turn to these global forums, particularly economic ones, which have been shaped by Western nations and in which China typically is a participant rather than a leader. Its record is one of responsibility: a player who is sometimes supportive and sometimes a critical second-guesser of actions agreed by others. Such behaviour is not unique; during the Great Depression the United States showed similar reluctance to lead in the urgent tasks of economic stabilization, largely because it had not thought through such a role for itself. China is in a similar position today.

In Chapter 7 I suggest a cooperative policy agenda for the two governments and their militaries. Rivalry is inevitable as they pursue their national interests, but cooperation could be strengthened with a two-part strategy. One part is the "inside game" between governments, beginning with leaders' setting the tone, goals, and agenda and high-level officials' managing both the cooperative efforts and continuing differences. The strategy would include closer engagement through diplomacy and intergovernmental negotiating machineries, particularly in the military. Much work is also needed to facilitate bilateral trade and investment flows and to connect the two countries' business communities.

In Chapter 8 I turn to the other part of the strategy, the "outside game" in which the US and Chinese governments work with their own publics and with other countries. Getting Asia "right" is the top priority. Each should be able to make room for the other's interests as they participate in Asia's nascent institutions for security and economic cooperation and in regional trade negotiations. Public engagement can also be stepped up in many ways –indeed, without their cooperation it will be impossible to implement global agreements on climate change, the use of outer space, and the increasingly fraught arena of cyberspace.

The book concludes with Chapter 9. An encouraging feature of the two presidents' Sunnylands meeting in 2013 was their vow to continue such informal meetings to foster cooperation between the established power and the rising power even as they pursue their national interests competitively. In the last chapter, therefore, I summarize what we should be looking for in the months and years ahead as mileposts along the road to developing the "habit" of cooperation as the two nations conduct their relationship. I also illustrate what is at stake in a hypothetical scenario of antagonism in which leaders are distracted from wise foreign policies that serve their countries' long-term interests. Occasional misunderstandings, volatility, and crises are inevitable, but the US-Chinese relationship will be central to managing the world economy in the decades ahead. Developing and managing a cooperative approach will be hard work, but far superior to the consequences of continuing the two countries' recent drift towards mistrust and antagonism.

1 The Changing Shape of the World Economy

The size of China's displacement of the world balance is such that the world must find a new balance. It is not possible to pretend that this is just another big player. This is the biggest player in the history of the world.

– Lee Kuan Yew[1]

A member of China's military was among the guests as China Central Television broadcast from Tiananmen Square in Beijing in November 2012. When asked about the reasons for the double-digit annual growth in China's military spending in recent years, his answer was, in effect, "that is what a Great Power does." Is China a Great Power? Singapore's former prime minister Lee Kuan Yew sees China as the biggest player in history. But size is only part of the story.

China's growth and dynamism have indeed reshaped the world economy, with the past decade a likely turning point. In 2000 the United States was indisputably the world's largest national economy, growing at close to 4 per cent a year, but the global financial crisis triggered in 2008 slowed the growth of all the large economies – in the decade to 2010 US annual growth averaged just 2 per cent, while Japan's and Germany's economies stagnated. China, meanwhile, sailed along, its growth exceeding 10 per cent a year (see Table 1.1). Measured in terms of purchasing power parity, the size of China's economy in 2010 was more than double Japan's and 70 per cent that of the United States. China now has the

Table 1.1. Comparisons of Gross Domestic Product: China, Japan, Germany, and United States, 2000 and 2010

	GDP[a]		Purchasing Power Parity GDP[a]		GDP Growth[b]	Purchasing Power Parity GDP per capita[c]	
	(US$ trillions)		(US$ trillions)		(% compound annual growth rate)	(US$)	
	2000	2010	2000	2010	2000–10	2000	2010
China	1.2	5.9	3.0	10.1	10.5	2,667	6,819
Japan	4.7	5.5	3.3	4.3	0.7	28,889	30,965
Germany	1.9	3.3	2.1	3.1	0.9	30,298	33,565
United States	9.9	14.4	9.9	14.4	1.6	39,545	42,079

[a] Values for respective years are based on current US dollars.
[b] Growth rates are based on constant 2000 US dollars.
[c] Values are based on constant 2005 international dollars.
Source: World Bank, available online at http://data.worldbank.org.

world's largest market for vehicles, a growing role in world trade, and the largest number of Internet users; it is also the world's largest emitter of carbon dioxide (see Table 1.2). As well, the size of its military spending is second only to that of the United States – although still only 24 per cent of the US level. China holds the world's largest stock of foreign-exchange reserves, and in 2012 PetroChina and the Industrial and Commercial Bank of China were ranked third and sixth, respectively, on the *Financial Times* Global 500 list of the world's largest public companies.

Until the global financial crisis the United States was unquestionably in charge following the collapse of central planning in the late 1980s, the implosion of the Soviet Union, and the end of the Cold War. Although an unanticipated rise in US house prices set off the crisis, the fire was already smouldering as a result of relaxed lending standards and financial innovations that diffused into international markets, adding systemic risks that regulators, chief executive officers, and boards of directors failed to understand or anticipate. The financial crisis became a classic case of debt-driven collapse. In October 2012 the International Monetary Fund pointed out in its *World Economic Outlook* that the amount of indebtedness in Japan, the United States, and several European countries was larger than the size of their entire economies.[2]

Adjusting to and overcoming the crisis has been a painful process, both economically and politically. In the United States, adjustments have been delayed by intense political polarization, a political gridlock that is not unprecedented in US history – the recent popular film *Lincoln* vividly portrays the political rancour over the role and size of government in the 1860s that is reminiscent of today's bitter arguments. In the globalized world of the twenty-first century, however, the policy and institutional failures that caused the financial crisis and the lack of political will to fix the problems have damaged both the leadership position of the United States and the soft power that flows from its innovative, dynamic, and efficient economic and financial systems.

European growth, too, was badly hit as governments moved to rescue failing banks. The causal factors differed from those in the United States in that European governments are expected to play

Table 1.2. Comparative Indicators: China, Japan, Germany, and United States

Indicator	China	Japan	Germany	United States
Merchandise exports, 2010 (US$ trillions)	1.6	0.8	1.3	1.3
Total trade, 2010[a] (US$ trillions)	1.8	0.8	1.5	1.8
Exports/GDP, 2010[a,b] (%)	29.5	15.2	46.8	12.7
Total trade/GDP, 2010[b] (%)	55.2	29.2	88.2	29.0
CO_2 emissions, 2008 (billions of metric tons)	7.0	1.2	0.8	5.5
CO_2 emissions, 2008 (metric tons per capita)	5.3	9.5	9.6	18.0
Number of Internet users, 2010 (per 100 people)	38	79	83	78
Number of Internet users, 2010 (millions)	514	100	68	242
Population, 2010 (millions)	1,338	127	82	309
Automobiles, 2011 (millions)	14.5	7.2	5.9	3.0
Commercial vehicles, 2011 (millions)	3.9	1.2	0.4	5.7
Total, 2011 (millions)	18.4	8.4	6.3	8.7
Defence spending, 2012 (constant 2012 US$ billions)	166	59	46	682

[a] Total trade includes goods and services.

[b] Available values for respective years are based on current US dollars.

Sources: World Bank; Organisation Internationale des Constructeurs d'Automobiles, available online at http://oica.net/category/production-statistics; Stockholm Peace Research Institute, available online at http://www.sipri.org/research/armaments/milex/milex_database/milex_database.

a much greater role in the economy and in the provision of a social safety net. But the crisis also exposed key institutional and design flaws in the structure of the European Union. Without a fiscal union to complement the monetary union's single interest rate and currency, governments that lacked German discipline ran loose fiscal policies. Now, Germany's insistence on austerity and its unwillingness to import more from its EU partners or to tolerate a higher inflation rate is prolonging the pain. Nevertheless, European governments are committed to maintaining the Union, regardless of the cost. They are moving slowly towards deeper integration to include banking union and closer fiscal policy coordination, both of which will require them to cede more sovereignty to Brussels. Europe is a picture of slow adjustment that is likely to continue for at least the next decade.

By 2012, half a decade after the crisis began, European politicians were preoccupied with internal challenges. The US economy was returning to healthier real growth and housing prices were recovering, but business enthusiasm to borrow, invest, and hire remains subdued in the face of persistent political disagreements and uncertainties about fiscal and financial sector policies and the role of government. With these internal preoccupations, who will step forward to manage future global crises? In the decade before the crisis the US consumer was the world's growth engine; now it seems unlikely that increasingly constrained emerging markets will take up the challenge.

Although China's economy is slowing from its recent 10 per cent annual average rate of growth, it is still growing far faster than that of the United States. If, as seems likely, this growth differential continues in the years ahead, the two economies inevitably will converge in size (Figure 1.1). At its current annual growth rate of around 7 per cent, China's economy will double in size in ten years, while the US economy, at its current 2 per cent growth rate, will double in size in as many as thirty-five years. Along the way, the Chinese economy will exceed, on nearly any measure, the size of the US economy. When economists at Goldman Sachs first raised this possibility in their 2003 study of the so-called BRICs (Brazil, Russia, India, and China), they estimated that China would catch

Figure 1.1. The Comparative Growth of the United States, China, Japan, and Germany, 1970–2010 (constant US$ trillions)

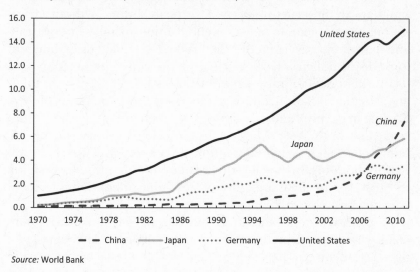

Source: World Bank

up with the United States around 2041; they now think this will happen as soon as 2026.[3]

China's growing economic influence could have profound implications for the way the world economy functions and the way it is governed. What will be China's stance towards the mandates and behaviour of global institutions? What will be the goals and intentions of its new leaders, who have not expressed much of a world view? Some predict that China, given its historical view of itself as the Middle Kingdom and its distinctive institutions, will seek to change, rather than support, the existing global order.

Historians remind us of earlier economic transitions, such as that between Britain and the United States after the First World War, when US policies took advantage of Britain's liberal trading policies. Yet the United States then shrank from assuming a role in global governance until after the Second World War, when it became deeply involved in the architecture of global financial institutions, financed the Marshall Plan that sped post-war Europe's economic recovery, and created the security umbrella of the North Atlantic Treaty Organization. Then, in the 1980s, it seemed as though another economic transition was taking place as Japan's rapid investment- and export-led post-war growth saw that country's economy rise to challenge that of the United States. Japanese policy mistakes, however, as well as institutional rigidities – including the world's most rapidly aging population and reluctance to encourage immigration or female participation in the labour force, or to raise the retirement age – have contributed to a decades-long economic stagnation from which Japan has yet to recover.[4]

Today, with the world's largest economies preoccupied with domestic rebalancing, is any major power able and willing to stabilize the world economy? The late Charles Kindleberger, the influential author of *Manias, Panics, and Crashes*,[5] implicitly assumed that only large countries would be able, although not always willing and committed, to play such a role. They produce such global public goods as an open trading system and freely flowing capital, are lenders of last resort in the event of financial crises, maintain a structure of exchange rates, and coordinate macroeconomic policies. If the largest countries will not do these things, then other countries need to step up and cooperate on agreed regimes of norms, rules, and decision-making procedures to shape expectations. But such cooperative structures can be unstable if free riders accept the benefits of stability without necessarily adhering to the regime that makes stability possible.

If and when China's becomes the world's largest economy, will China free ride or be willing to play a stabilizing role? Kindleberger's "large" countries tended to be relatively wealthy, with sophisticated economic decision-making structures and an appreciation of the value of international public goods. But China, although large, does not fit such a description. It is still relatively poor, and despite its growing and dynamic economy, it has a huge population to bring along. China, moreover, continues to be preoccupied by its own development and, like Western economies, faces major challenges of adjustment.

Some Chinese explain the influence of the country's long history on its thinking in a stylized way, citing three "historical Chinas":

five thousand years of traditional China as the Middle Kingdom, reaching a zenith between 1500 and 1800; five hundred years of living in a Western-centred world; and re-emerging only in the past fifty years with a new image and capabilities.[6] They see today's China as prosperous, respected, in possession of a strong military, and with a seat at the world's top tables.

China's venerable history further suggests a view of itself – although it is changing as more Chinese travel abroad – as that of a relatively closed, poor agrarian economy with strong material priorities and a value system that is hierarchical and conformist. To see this, one need only consider the apparent contradiction between China's spectacular economic growth and its modest implications for the average Chinese. It is true that, despite its huge population, China's macroeconomic miracle has translated into an average per capita income of nearly US$7,000, measured in terms of purchasing power parity. With household consumption estimated at 34 per cent of gross domestic product (GDP), however, this further translates into annual average per capita spending of around US$2,300. Compare this with household consumption in the United States of 70 per cent of GDP – or US$30,000 annually per capita – or even Brazil, where consumer spending is 61 per cent of GDP.

China's weak household consumption is a consequence of policy choices that favour producers over consumers. The transition from central planning and government ownership to a more market-driven economic structure is still on-going, and major areas of the economy remain in the hands of the state. Party cadres, 83 million strong, who administer economic and political activities reaching from the centre down to the villages, are assigned growth goals on which they are evaluated and promoted. In those industrial sectors deemed major contributors to strategic and economic security, state-owned enterprises (SOEs) have monopoly status protected by high entry barriers. They benefit from subsidized input prices, including those for capital and energy. Administered interest rates, set by the central bank but approved by the State Council, provide artificially cheap capital to the SOEs and large corporations that are the banks' major borrowers. Labour markets are flexible, allowing employers considerable freedom to hire and fire, but they are distorted by the *hukou* household registration system, which restricts the movement of rural workers and their families to the cities. Moreover, discrimination against families that *hukou* registers as rural denies them and their children access to education and social services available to families with urban registration. Millions of jobs have been created and millions of people lifted out of poverty, but as more Chinese approach lower-middle-class living standards, the distortions and costs of the approach are widely recognized as unsustainable.

The opportunity costs and unintended consequences of allocating resources in this way are becoming more apparent. Administered prices for coal, oil, and natural gas that maintain them below those in world markets are costly to the coal- and petroleum-producing interior provinces, which are denied the full value of their resources. The cheap credit available to SOEs is used too generously, raising the capital intensity of what is still a labour-abundant economy, undermining job creation and raising unemployment above what it otherwise would be.[7] The implications of such distortions and waste are more serious as growth slows since they implicitly penalize the non-state sector, which tends to be more efficient and productive.[8]

Today, China is one of the world's more unequal economies. Graphic illustrations of this inequality can be found on the streets of Beijing and Shanghai, where on busy roads Porches and Maseratis pass hawkers and vendors with laden bicycles or carts drawn by draught animals. Economists use a measure called the Gini coefficient to determine income inequality (the proportion of income accruing to each income decile), where 1 denotes complete inequality, with all income going to a single person, and 0.4 is seen as the threshold for potential social unrest. In China since 1980, that measure has risen from 0.3 to an official figure of 0.474,[9] meaning that income inequality is lower in China than in Brazil or South Africa but above the United States or even India. In terms of concentration of wealth, however, China is estimated to have ninety-five billionaires with a joint net worth of 2.6 per cent of GDP, far less unequal than Russia, where ninety-six billionaires' net worth is equivalent to 18.6 per cent of GDP, or India, whose forty-eight billionaires' net worth is 10.9 per cent of GDP (although under-reporting is possible).[10]

CHINA'S STRUCTURAL CHALLENGES

China will have to address these distortions. As it moves beyond mobilizing capital and labour to drive export-led growth, it will have to rely more heavily on domestic demand. That, in turn, will require reducing income inequality, encouraging the growth of middle-class households, and relying more on their consumption for growth to offset reliance on exports to US and European markets.

With restructuring, China's production, employment, and incomes will change.[11] Weaker export markets will mean falling demand for machinery and equipment and for manufactured goods. Higher consumption will shift domestic demand towards services relative to investment and exports, encouraging growth and higher productivity in the services sectors. Shares of national income will also change as household consumption rises in response to higher incomes and the increasing provision of public services for health and education.

Such a shift will require both policy and institutional changes. I examine these in more detail in Chapter 3, but they include tax cuts and more government spending on social programs to reduce high rates of precautionary saving. Enterprises will have to pay more in dividend income to their government owners, which means they will have less to save and the national savings-investment imbalance will decline.[12] Deregulating interest rates will raise household incomes, while greater exchange-rate flexibility – allowing the Chinese currency to appreciate against other currencies – will benefit households directly by making imports cheaper and indirectly by removing the main reason for administering interest rates. Some changes have already begun – for example, the introduction of cooperative medical insurance, partial reimbursement of health costs, and rural pension programs, and the elimination of school meals for primary school students in rural areas.[13]

In short, the economic prescription for restructuring is straight-forward. But there is considerable uncertainty about how success-ful implementation will be because of resistance from enterprises, including SOEs, with economic power and influence and from individuals with family and political privilege. The risk of allowing the status quo to continue, however, is greater and could soon out-weigh the political risk. "Business as usual" in the form of corrupt practices and government's autocracy is increasingly subject to vo-cal criticism. Well-known artist Ai Weiwei, who helped design the famous Bird's Nest stadium for the 2008 Beijing Olympics, is one of the most vocal and unrepentant critics. In 2011 he was detained by the public security bureau and his disappearance for eighty-one days attracted global attention, highlighting the Chinese gov-ernment's sensitivity to potential social unrest. Upon release he was fined US$2.4 million for alleged tax evasion and forbidden to leave the country for a year. Also active are bloggers such as Hung Huang, a fashion magazine publisher in Beijing, who is well known for her self-censored but blunt commentaries on wealth and power. With an estimated six million followers, she represents a new phenomenon in China: an independent commentator who speaks up from outside the official media.[14] With half a billion Chinese using the Internet and an estimated 100 million daily us-ers of the micro-blogging site Sina Weibo, many Chinese are now relatively well informed about events. They also have increasing access not only to opinion, but to information as well – including information provided by some municipal and provincial govern-ment Web sites – and are becoming more informed about dispari-ties in income and power.

Indeed, corruption has become a sufficiently major concern within the Party leadership that both the outgoing and incoming leaders identified it as a priority. Hu Jintao, at the beginning of his thirty-eight-page work report to the November 2012 Party Con-gress, warned that, "[s]ome sectors are prone to corruption and other misconduct, and the fight against corruption remains a seri-ous challenge for us. We must take these difficulties and problems very seriously and work harder to resolve them."[15] In his first pub-lic comments as the new leader, Xi Jinping said, "In the new situation, our party faces many severe challenges, and there are many pressing problems within the party that need to be resolved, especially problems such as corruption and bribe-taking by some party members and cadres, being out of touch with the people, placing undue emphasis on formality and bureaucracy must be addressed with great effort."[16] Prior to the 2013 spring festival holidays, Xi ordered official restraint in gift giving and entertaining and more attention to getting in touch with the people, a welcome gesture. His assigning Wang Qishan, an experienced, no-nonsense and senior leader, to be secretary of the Party's Central Commission for Discipline Inspection suggests that officials will be held more accountable for their behaviour, but this in itself will not remove the institutional distortions and incentives that are at the root of the problem.

IMPLEMENTING STRUCTURAL REFORMS

An overarching characteristic of the Chinese political system is its lack of transparency and the absence of checks and balances that in Western democracies are commonly provided by legislatures, elections, and the courts. This leaves gaps in property rights within which patronage relationships and networks form. Those seeking security for their property enter into alliances with those with political power, exchanging favours for security from expropriation, while those with power are able to access investment, credit, and land.

Structural reforms, however, will be hard to achieve. Cautious conservatives favour social reforms over the difficult moves needed to rein in the state sector, introduce market forces into investment and production decisions, and restructure the government-owned financial system. In the face of such conservatism, the logical way to proceed would be to begin with the less controversial reforms – further support for consumption and investments in human capital – that would have wide public support.

One possible road map to reform is *China 2030*, a joint study by the World Bank and the Development Research Center of the State Council, published in 2012 and endorsed by Premier Li Keqiang.[17] It recommends beginning with investments in human capital, encouraging opportunities for public participation in the reform process, and developing indicators by which progress can be evaluated and measured. It also suggests focusing on "quick wins" that address short-term risks, most notably by deregulating interest rates and allowing household incomes the benefits of higher deposit rates, increasing dividend payments to the treasury from SOEs, replacing forced land acquisitions with a transparent, market-based process of payment (and taxation), raising the retirement age, and introducing free secondary education in rural areas.

Leaders' speeches at the November 2012 Party Congress indicated some desire to move in these directions. Following Deng Xiaoping's 1992 precedent, a southern tour by Xi Jinping was also seen as a signal of his commitment to reform. In February 2013 the State Council released an information circular on a new income equality plan aimed at boosting living standards. It included expanding property taxation, increasing spending on social safety net programs and income transfers, including migrant workers in the pension system, and accelerating the introduction of a universal health care system. The circular also called for respect for the property rights of rural land owners and improvements in the land registration system. But such reforms will take time to implement.[18] Phasing out the *hukou* household registration system and introducing more competition into the enterprise sector will be particularly difficult. Opposition from powerful and wealthy SOEs is already evident; additional opposition can also be expected from workers in protected but uncompetitive enterprises and in polluting industries. Once the road to reform is taken and as political consensus for travelling it is built, however, it should be easier to obtain the cooperation of vested interests and to begin to dismantle some of the tougher obstacles to the ongoing development of a market economy.

DEEPENING INTERDEPENDENCE

Given China's domestic preoccupations, the speed of its rise to economic pre-eminence in the wake of the global financial crisis has been a surprise. China is now a major player in the world trad-

Table 1.3. China as a Major Trading Partner, 2011*

Country	Exports to China (% of total exports)	Imports from China (% of total imports)	Total trade with China (US$ billions)
United States	7	18	521
Hong Kong	54	43	467
Japan	20	21	346
South Korea	24	16	221
Taiwan	28	14	126
Australia	28	19	111
Brazil	17	14	77
India	6	12	72
Canada	4	11	66
Mexico	2	15	58
Malaysia	13	13	55

*Includes merchandise trade only.
Sources: United Nations, Comtrade database; source for Taiwan is United States, Central Intelligence Agency, The World Factbook (Washington, DC: Central Intelligence Agency, 2012), available online at https://www.cia.gov/library/publications/the-world-factbook/index.html.

ing system: the value of its trade with its top six trading partners was almost US$2 trillion in 2011 (see Table 1.3), or more than an eighth of the world total.[19] The United States is China's largest national market by far, while its trade with neighbouring Japan, South Korea, and Taiwan accounts for more than 20 per cent of their exports or imports. Natural resources suppliers such as Brazil, Australia, and Malaysia are also heavily dependent on Chinese demand.

Although China accounts for relatively smaller shares of US exports and imports, for a short time prior to the 2008 crisis it surpassed Canada, traditionally the United States' largest trading partner, as the top source of imports. The deepening US-Chinese economic interdependence is also apparent in China's holdings of US Treasury securities, which peaked at a 25 per cent share in 2011 according to US Treasury estimate (Figure 1.2); also by that year China had accumulated more than US$3 trillion in foreign-exchange reserves (Table 1.4). China, of course, continues to hold these US securities because of their credibility in global financial

Figure 1.2. China's Holdings of US Treasury Bonds, 2001–13 (US$ billions)

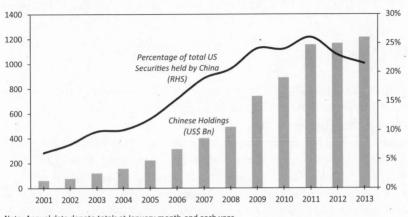

Note: Annual data denote totals at January month-end each year.
Historical data: http://www.treasury.gov/resource-center/data-chart-center/tic/Documents/mfhhis01.txt
Monthly data, current year: http://www.treasury.gov/resource-center/data-chart-center/tic/Documents/mfh.txt
Source: US Department of the Treasury

Table 1.4. China's Foreign-Exchange Reserves, 2005–12

	Amount (US$ billions)	Annual Growth Rate (%)
2005	819	34
2006	1,066	30
2007	1,528	43
2008	1,946	27
2009	2,399	23
2010	2,847	19
2011	3,181	12
2012 (June)	3,240	

Source: China, State Administration of Foreign Exchange, available
online at http://www.safe.gov.cn.

markets. Indeed, as the global crisis deepened in 2008, along with
the repatriation of capital by cash-strapped US corporations, capital flowed into US securities as a safe haven in sufficient volume to
strengthen the US dollar. With few alternatives in global financial
markets and with China determined to invest its foreign-exchange

reserves only in foreign assets, the stage is set for the economic interdependence of China and the United States to continue to deepen.

WHO WILL LEAD?

China's rise is reshaping the world economy. As measured by purchasing power parity, China's economy is now 70 per cent that of the United States, and its economic growth rate is four times higher. It has twice as many Internet users and produces five times as many cars as the United States. It is now one of world's most open economies and the top goods exporter. Some of these metrics will be modified as China rebalances its economy, reduces carbon emissions, raises per capita incomes – which still average only 10 per cent of those of Americans; its per capita consumption is even smaller – and reduces income inequality.

The sheer size of these metrics and the depth of economic interdependence they convey drive external expectations. Less evident to outsiders are the internal contradictions that China's leaders must address. Jobs have been delivered and incomes raised, but at substantial long-term cost. Artificially low input prices distort production and investment decisions. Failure to enforce environmental regulations permits pollution of air, land, and water, causing enormous health and cleanup costs. Producers are favoured while households are burdened, many with choices restricted by their rural birthplaces. The Party delivers competent meritocratic administration, but Party members and their families getting rich because of privilege rather than through their own effort feeds resentment and anger, not wealth creation. These costly and evident distortions undermine China's projection of soft power and its potential role in managing economic shocks, military conflicts, or outbreaks of contagious diseases. They lessen its influence on others to change their behaviour, and they raise a more practical question: can Chinese officials who have studied only in China and advanced through China's merit-based but transactional patronage system provide leadership in the more objective and technocratic systems found in international institutions?

By default, it seems, the United States will continue to lead the international system, but more as "leader of last resort," as some have called it, providing ideas, support, and rhetorical guidance more than the financial resources to act.[20] Yet, largely because of the evolving world economy, more is expected of China in the way of financial contributions and ideas for international institutions and coalitions of the willing. So far, its contributions to international public goods, such as stepping up foreign aid in parts of developing Asia and Africa and halting piracy in the Arabian Sea, have been made largely to advance its own interests.

China's leaders, then, will have to set the country on the road to serious economic restructuring, but bedevilling their attempts to do so will be China's profound demographic challenges – most particularly its aging population – to which I turn in the next chapter.

2 China's Incomplete Transformation, or What It Means to Age before Becoming Rich

Chris Patten, during his tenure as Hong Kong's last British administrator in the mid-1990s, observed that "China will grow old before it is rich." Trite as it might sound today, although it is on a trajectory to becoming the world's largest economy, with all that implies in terms of geopolitics, China is still relatively poor. That is how many Chinese think of themselves. The thirty-year-old one-child policy has been notably successful in banishing the Malthusian spectre of the population's outstripping available resources, yet even three decades of rapid economic growth have seen real per capita income in China rise only as high as the lower-middle-income level among the world's nations. When the ratio of elderly dependents to the working population in advanced economies such as the United States, Japan, and South Korea was at the level projected for China in 2020, real per capita incomes in those countries were three to six times higher than China's are expected to be.[1]

When there are more people of working age than the number who depend on them, a demographic dividend occurs in terms of faster growth. This positive relationship between demographic change and economic growth is illustrated dramatically in a 2000 study showing that the demographic dividend contributed between a third and a half of East Asia's growth "miracle" in the period between 1965 and 1990 period.[2] Eventually, however, the dividend from this youthful age structure dissipates as fertility rates decline with social and economic development.

Figure 2.1. China's Dependency Ratio and Population Growth, 1950–2100

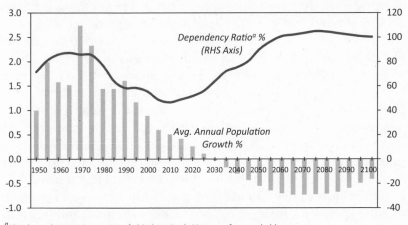

^aThe dependency ratio consists of elderly retired, 60 years of age and older
Source: http://esa.un.org/unpd/wpp/unpp/panel_indicators.htm

DEMOGRAPHIC CHANGES

China is aging and its demographic dividend is disappearing. Annual population growth rates are declining and the number of fifteen-to-twenty-four-year-olds entering the labour force is beginning to shrink. The United Nations projects that, between 2010 and 2030, China's productive population – those between the ages of fifteen and fifty-nine[3] – will decline from 68 to 61 per cent of the total, while the number of those over age sixty will increase to 25 per cent of the total, or 340 million, larger than the entire populations of most countries (see Figure 2.1).

The decline in the China's working-age population will have three significant implications: a rising dependency ratio, a shrinking labour force, and a negative effect on economic growth that will have to be offset by rising productivity.

A rising dependency ratio: The dependency ratio is simply the ratio of the young and the elderly to the productive population – in other words, those outside the labour force must be supported by those within it. Traditionally, Chinese families have taken care of aging parents – even during the time of Mao Zedong communal living arrangements in state enterprises and urban and rural communes, known as the "iron rice bowl," provided for all living needs. Now, however, the family structure is changing. Tens of millions of rural migrant workers spend all but a few weeks a year away from their single children, who remain at their birthplace to be reared by grandparents, other older relatives, or even neighbours. Children do not join their parents in the cities as they would in other countries because of China's *hukou* system of household registration. Is the parent-child attachment sufficiently strong for children to shoulder the financial obligations of parents they hardly know? Demands for social programs and publicly financed pensions are growing, but without adequate public funding households must increase their precautionary saving to fund their needs themselves. Fortunately, since demographic shifts are very slow as seen from the perspective of the household, savings are unlikely to decline for some time, an issue to which I return below.

A shrinking labour force. China's labour force is shrinking as each year fewer young people are seeking to enter. According to the United Nations, the number of fifteen-to-twenty-four-year-olds increased from 196 million in 2000 to 225 million in 2010, but is projected to return to 2000 levels by 2015 and to continue to drop to 158 million by 2030. These smaller numbers for this cohort will mean that the central objective of creating jobs can be achieved with less growth. Labour costs, however, will be under pressure – just how much pressure depends on the allocation of labour, and is a matter of controversy. Most economists argue that nearly 100 million people remain underemployed in rural agriculture, and that their movement out of that sector will continue to exert downward pressure on wages.[4] Others disagree, arguing that these people are employed in rural non-agricultural activities and most are over age forty, and that encouraging them to migrate to urban jobs would only cause wages to rise even higher.[5] In the more advanced coastal provinces, workers' protests and a growing scarcity of migrant labour have exacerbated the effects of labour force shrinkage. The government has responded by introducing and enforcing minimum wage and other labour legislation, but rising labour costs are chipping away at China's traditional comparative advantage of abundant supplies of low-cost labour. As the residual rural labour pool disappears, the powerful growth momentum from moving labour out of low-productivity activities into more productive but low-wage employment in urban areas is also fading. To maintain growth the economy must rely more heavily on using labour more efficiently and shift to growth driven less by labour and more by capital, knowledge, and productivity, required significant institutional changes.

Slower economic growth: The effects of a declining working-age population on future economic growth are less certain. The shrinking labour force puts pressure on costs, but these can be offset by a labour force that is more productive. China's productivity growth is relatively robust – by one calculation, if current increases in total factor productivity (the efficiency with which all inputs are combined) were to continue for the next two decades, China's productivity level would still be only 40 per cent that of the United States, implying substantial room for future gains.[6] So far, most of these gains have depended on the mobilization of rural labour; going forward, the task will include improving labour skills and education. In fact, for its level of development, China's labour force is already quite well educated, and labour productivity grew rapidly between 1990 and 2010, averaging more than 8 per cent annually (Figure 2.2). Labour productivity is still well below levels in the United States, however, indicating there is much room for further improvement.

CHINA'S POLICY AGENDA

The prospects for productivity growth imply that China's policy agenda must focus first on meeting the needs of the dependent population. Abandoning the one-child policy is also under discussion, and the existing labour supply can be used more efficiently

Figure 2.2. China's Productivity Performance in International Perspective, 1990 and 2010

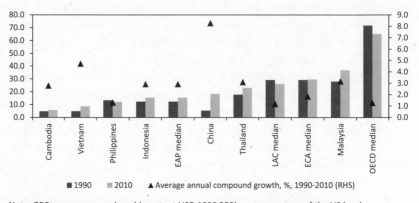

■ 1990   ■ 2010   ▲ Average annual compound growth, %, 1990-2010 (RHS)

Note: GDP per person employed (constant USD 1990 PPP) as a percentage of the US level
Data sources: ILO Key Indicators of the Labor Market; World Bank staff calculations
Sources: World Bank, *East Asia and Pacific Economic Update,* May 2012, available at
http://data.worldbank.org/data-catalog/eap-economic-update.

by stepping up urbanization and abolishing the discriminatory *hukou* household registration system.

Financing Dependents

China has made considerable progress in creating pension, health, and social security services, but how is it now to pay for them? The most popular revenue source is the large and profitable state-owned enterprises (SOEs) that have been exempted since the 1990s from paying dividends, both to repair their balance sheets and to give their managers the competitive advantage of access to low-cost capital. Since 2007 the State Council has gradually increased the dividend rate for profitable enterprises (except those that produce military armaments), but instead of the funds being channelled into general revenues for social uses, they have been earmarked for a capital budget that channels them back to the SOEs, an issue to which I return in Chapter 3.[7]

Abandoning the One-Child Policy

China's primary driver of demographic change has been the one-child policy. Demographic studies have explored the effects on population size and demographic structure of various options for easing and eventually abandoning the policy.[8] But will parents actually choose larger families if permitted? As theory suggests and empirical studies show, couples choose to have fewer children as incomes rise with economic development. Instead they tend to invest more in fewer children, improving their skills and preparing them for more promising futures than would be possible if family size were larger.[9] The case for large families is most compelling in agrarian societies as a hedge against high infant mortality rates and the loss of children as potential economic assets as agricultural workers and as care-givers for elderly dependents. These arguments lose their force, however, in a modern environment of low infant mortality and monetized economic relationships.

In recent years the one-child policy and its enforcement have varied widely across the country. The Shanghai government, for example, permits parents who themselves are single children to have two. In other major urban areas, however, parents of a second child are required to pay a fine that varies with their economic circumstances. In still other areas, mothers have been forced to abort a second pregnancy. The National Population and Family Planning Commission, which employs half a million full-time and six million part-time employees, collects millions of yuan per year from parents who violate the policy.[10] One signal that the policy might be eased was the decision, ratified by the 2013 National Peoples' Congress, to merge the Commission with the Ministry of Health as part of a larger bureaucratic streamlining, and to shift its mandate to "family development."[11]

A related issue of increasing social importance is the stark gender imbalance associated with the one-child policy: the 2000 census revealed that the sex ratio at birth had risen to 117 males for every 100 females. Many outside observers see this imbalance as a source of social tension. One indicator is the marriage market, which has become a "sellers" market for young women and their families whose minimum economic demands of a suitor and his family are a job, a car, and an apartment. Another, more troubling indicator is the increasing number of stories of child abduction, as parents desperate for a son turn to child traffickers. A third indicator is location: much of the burden of the gender imbalance is borne by rural males who lack the skills and education needed to compete in the marriage market.[12]

Using Existing Labour More Efficiently

China's transition to productivity-driven growth will require upgrading the skills and knowledge of its labour force. The authorities, recognizing the importance of such human capital investments, have set ambitious goals in the Twelfth Five-Year Plan to increase the number of university graduates and to step up the pace of innovation by investing in world-class research facilities at leading universities, in R&D infrastructure, and in research clusters that nurture private start-up firms and interact with industrial sectors. Anecdotal evidence, however, indicates that many university graduates are unable to find jobs, while many employers are unable to find workers with the technical skills they need. A greater emphasis on vocational training would help, as would flexible programs to use older workers and enhanced opportunities for mid-career skills training. Benefits such as pensions should be made portable to increase labour mobility within urban locations.

Increasing Urbanization

Most of these human capital opportunities will be found in urban areas. Just over 50 per cent of China's population is now urban (Figure 2.3), but considering its aging population, that is a much lower level than in either Germany or Japan, two other large and aging economies, because of China's legacy of restrictions on rural-to-urban migration. China's urban population is optimistically projected to rise to a billion people by 2030, with 221 cities over

Figure 2.3. China's Urban Population, 1953–2012 (millions)

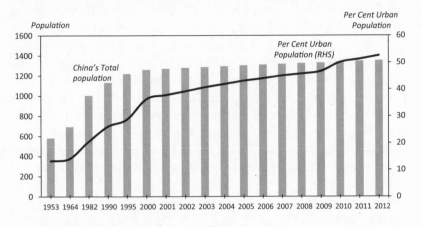

Source: China's National Bureau of Statistics
http://www.stats.gov.cn/english/statisticaldata/otherdata/men&women_en.pdf
http://www.stats.gov.cn/english/newsandcomingevents/t20120120_402780233.htm
http://www.stats.gov.cn/english/statisticaldata/otherdata/brics2011/P020110412519191303418.pdf
http://www.stats.gov.cn/english/pressrelease/t20130222_402874590.htm

one million each.[13] Such a prediction assumes, however, continued economic growth fuelled by massive investments in real estate and infrastructure and in services that spur personal consumption and economic growth by attracting talent, investment, and the creation of network effects. It is also estimated that as many as 500 million jobs will be in cities, attracting migrants who could account for more than 40 per cent of the urban population by 2025.[14]

More investment by itself, however, is not the answer. Urban jobs and infrastructure by themselves will not increase consumption. Institutional changes are required, including legally contestable leasing arrangements for urban housing. Sustainable long-term growth also depends on institutional changes to raise low levels of productivity in the services industries and, to encourage competition and job creation, the deregulation of these industries, many of which – such as transport, logistics, tourism and entertainment, community services, health, and education

– are still monopolized by the state. Financing the provision of a social safety net for China's estimated 220-to-250 million migrant workers is also required to reduce their high propensity to save.[15] Premier Li Keqiang has become a champion of urbanization as a way to achieve better-quality growth. He advocates financing the transformation by creating municipal bonds to be guaranteed by the central government. Until the transparent and rules-based financial infrastructure is in place for such long-term transactions, however, there is a risk that the government will press funding on banks whose asset quality has already been undermined by government-directed lending since the global financial crisis.

Phasing Out Hukou

Hukou, the household registration system, affects the more efficient use of China's shrinking labour force. It is discriminatory, promotes inequality, and has outlived its original purpose of regulating urban migration in a subsistence agricultural economy. Although restrictions on population movement now have been largely eliminated, entitlements to education and social services in the cities are still denied to migrants. Such discrimination is even changing the family structure. The plight of an estimated 58 million children left behind in rural areas by their migrant parents is a troubling side effect periodically highlighted in the popular press. As one report noted, 15 November 2012 – the day Xi Jinping inherited the Party leadership – might have been a banner day at the Great Hall of the People, but it was one of tragedy for five "left-behind" boys in Bijie, Guizhou province. Their parents, migrant workers in Shenzhen, had left the five cousins with an elderly uncle. It was a cold night, and the boys sought warmth by sleeping in a dumpster. They made a fire to keep warm, and all five suffocated.[16]

A number of experiments are under way in different localities to turn *hukou* into a national population registration system. Shanghai has removed its restrictions based on birthplace, but rigorously rations changes from rural to urban registration to restrict total numbers admitted. Guangdong applies a scoring system to applications to convert to urban status. Chongqing allows the exchange of urban for rural status, but only for its own residents. Chengdu has experimented with temporary and permanent conversions, again open only to its own residents.[17] These experiments underline the need for a national system. The country as a whole stands to benefit from efficiencies realized by changes to the registration system, but because local governments bear the costs of reform, they restrict the numbers they are prepared to qualify.

One proposal is for a national conversion strategy to be phased in gradually, beginning with a framework in which the social entitlements of a locality's non-residents are de-linked from *hukou* status.[18] The ultimate goal would be the introduction of a residence permit that would give everyone who qualifies the same rights. Negotiations would be required, however, because the conversion would have to include financing services for elderly dependents and non-residents in urban areas. Another proposal is to experiment with two-track access to health, education, and social services, with full access initially available only to permanent residents, while newcomers initially would be able to access only certain services, such as basic education, expanding later to health care and other social services as public resources become available and newcomers' incomes rise.[19]

Phasing out *hukou* would require negotiating politically sensitive trade-offs with entrenched interests. Most analysts suggest that the central government finance social safety nets by increasing the dividends SOEs are required to remit, so the resistance of such enterprises would have to be overcome. Urban parents are another interest group opposed to eliminating *hukou*, since an influx of children of migrants, in their view, would serve only to increase the numbers of children registering to take the fiercely competitive college entrance exams known as *gaokao*.[20] These sources of resistance, however, would have to weighed against the reality that most migrants are unlikely to return to their own rural areas – although many workers from the interior who have moved to the coastal provinces do return to nearby towns and smaller cities to set up businesses of their own.

THE MIDDLE-INCOME TRAP

The implications of China's population structure highlight two issues. First, productivity growth needs to be encouraged to compensate for the diminishing effects of simply mobilizing the rural labour force. Second, labour resources need to be better used, rather than misallocated or underutilized as is often the case now. Ignoring such challenges could cause growth to slow. This dilemma, however, is not unique to China: international comparisons of developing countries reveal that, as they reach middle-income levels – around US$10,000 per capita on a constant dollar purchasing-power-parity basis – growth slows or stalls. The World Bank's Commission on Growth and Development has found that only thirteen developing countries have sustained high rates of growth throughout the period since the end of the Second World War. Brazil, Indonesia, Malaysia, and Thailand started strongly, but their growth rates slowed before per capita income reached high-income levels. China, however, is one of the thirteen, having sustained high growth since 1978, along with Hong Kong, Japan, South Korea, Singapore, and Taiwan.[21] Another study, by Barry Eichengreen et al. for the National Bureau of Economic Research, finds that the likelihood that growth will decelerate rises in economies with per capita income of US$10,000 and peaks at US$17,000.[22] This tendency for growth to slow or stagnate is called the "middle-income trap."

There is no single explanation for such a growth slowdown. The Commission on Growth and Development notes that countries that continued to grow to high-income levels had certain common policies: they opened up their economies, maintained macroeconomic stability and high rates of saving and investment, provided credible, committed, and capable government, and allowed markets to allocate resources. The study by Eichengreen et al. finds that the decline in rates of growth tends to be productivity related: growth slows as the efficiency with which capital and labour are used is eventually exhausted.

What both studies indicate is that slowdowns are the result of multiple factors that change the drivers of growth. Countries experience rapid growth as they move abundant supplies of low-cost labour to more productive employment and as they benefit from ready access to existing technologies through imports and foreign direct investment. This is the easy part. As these labour supplies dry up and wages rise, however, their exports lose competitiveness, and the hard part begins. Income gains slow unless other ways are found to improve productivity performance – by adopting better technologies, for example. The "trap" into which such middle-income countries fall is where they lose competitiveness relative to other low-wage, labour-abundant countries that are catching up to them, while they lack the differentiated products and services with which they can compete with high-income, more technologically sophisticated countries. To avoid the trap, governments of middle-income countries must anticipate the need to change policies and to foresee potential market failures in advance. Eichengreen et al., for example, find that countries with undervalued currencies and low consumer spending – two characteristics of the current Chinese economy – seem to be more vulnerable to slowdown.

China's challenge can be framed by a comparison of South Korea and Brazil. South Korea, one of the poorest countries in Asia at the end of the Korean War, had become a high-income member of the industrialized world by 2000. It success is attributed to such factors as its relatively equal income distribution, which produced a sizable middle class whose demand for education and consumer products drove its industrial diversification into services and knowledge-based industries. In the wake of the 1997 Asian financial crisis, the South Korean government introduced major institutional reforms, including its own withdrawal from production and ownership and instead assuming the role of setting the framework for the private sector. Over the years, major investments in the development of South Korea's education system have also been synchronized with its industrial growth.[23]

Brazil, in contrast, has fallen into the middle-income trap. Between 1945 and 1980 it experienced 7 per cent real growth as it exploited its large domestic market and plentiful agricultural resources. But income inequality was high and tolerated, and demand from the country's relatively small middle class failed to have much effect on industrial diversification. Brazil became highly indebted after the first oil price shock of the 1970s as it borrowed

heavily from abroad to finance its costly import-substitution industrialization. Exports declined, and growth dropped to an average
annual rate of 4 per cent between 2000 and 2010. Its education
system is inadequate to support a more productive labour force,
and ts saving and investment rates are much lower than China's,
while the share of GDP accounted for by consumption is twice as
high as in China.[24] Brazil has since restored balance to its public
accounts, adopted an inflation target, and freed up market forces,
but it still has much work to do to build its education system and
improve physical infrastructure.

China's leaders have committed to doubling per capita income
by 2020, which would take it to the US$12,000 level. There is,
however, no magic way to achieve such a goal. China will have to
change institutions and policies to encourage productivity growth
that exceeds wage growth. It will have to move beyond its reliance
on surplus labour from low-productivity activities in the countryside, and it will have to invest in the education and skills necessary
to ensure rising labour productivity in the modern sector. Reducing obstacles to labour mobility will help. Another factor will be
the growth of the middle class. Increasing household incomes will
increase domestic demand for goods and more efficient services,
which will take up the slack as export growth slows. Reducing income inequality is a related priority, which other middle-income
countries have tackled by making educational access and opportunity more equal, increasing household income by deregulating interest rates, and increasing access to credit for job-creating small
and medium-sized enterprises.[25]

Finally, as China ages before it becomes rich, its leaders face
rising expectations for a strong social safety net for the elderly.
Here again, change will not come overnight. Some experienced
analysts, having learned from Brazil's heavy spending and borrowing, counsel against "big bang" dramatic increases in social spending as potentially counterproductive and wasteful.[26] As the South
Korean case shows, anticipating necessary policy and institutional
changes to sustain growth requires leadership with political clout
and widespread public support. Will it take a crisis to make such
progress? I address this question in the next chapter.

3 Turning Point or Countdown to Crisis?

After more than 30 years of rapid growth, China has reached another turning point in its development path when a second strategic, and no less fundamental, shift is called for. The 12th Five Year Plan provides an excellent start.

— *China 2030*

The desire of acquiring the comforts of the world haunts the imagination of the poor, and the dread of losing them that of the rich.

— Alexis de Toqueville

China has made slow progress in addressing former premier Wen Jiabao's 2007 diagnosis of its economic model as unsustainable, uncoordinated, unbalanced, and unstable. The mobilization of rural labour has been a growth driver on the supply side, but going forward China faces twin challenges in moving onto a sustainable path to high per capita income. One challenge is to achieve further productivity gains on the supply side to stay ahead of wage gains. The other is to carry out the reforms necessary to raise domestic demand, beginning with modifying policies and institutions that favour producers over households, goods manufacturers over services, and investment over consumption.

Reforms are slowly moving in the right direction, but producers' input prices for energy, land, capital, and use of the environment continue to be subsidized. The services sector, moreover, has hardly grown: after expanding rapidly during the 1990s to account for 41.5 per cent of gross domestic product (GDP) by 2002, it since has stalled, reaching only 43 per cent of GDP by 2010.[1] Investment growth moderated somewhat between 2005 and 2007, but in 2010 its share of GDP, at 49 per cent, was still unusually high. Exchange-rate appreciation has made only a modest contribution to reducing the prices of imported goods. Personal income tax cuts have been modest. Changes in financial policies have been what Nicholas Lardy describes as "anemic."[2] Finally, increases in spending on a social safety net, health care expenditures, and pensions and payments to low-income families have been too modest to change consumption behaviour. Indeed, China's weak social safety net and high income inequality might have influenced household savings behaviour in the opposite direction: without Mao Zedong's "iron rice bowl," households have been left to fend for themselves and, as a result, have increased their precautionary saving. Low returns on these savings might have encouraged even more belt-tightening than if returns had been higher.

In the intense debates about economic restructuring, one sees both agreement on the direction of reform and disagreement on its pace and details. In a series of essays compiled by the European Council on Foreign Relations in 2012,[3] several scholars call for the return of the state in labour and capital markets to ensure higher wages and deposit rates at banks, to expand the social safety net, and to bring about *hukou* reform. Others, including pioneers of the original gradualist market reforms, advocate more supply-side reforms to finish the job by privatizing land and state enterprises and liberalizing the financial sector. All are concerned with vested interests opposed to reforms, but some argue that only a democratic-type of government can take on those interests, while others call for strong, charismatic leadership of the type that characterized Deng Xiaoping's rule to override opposition.[4]

The longer the delay in moving beyond the mobilization of inputs such as labour and capital and correcting demand-side distortions, the more difficult these distortions will be to remove. In turn this will reduce the country's long-term growth potential and increase the chances of painful adjustments forced by crisis. As in other fast-growing economies, in China mixed signals encourage corruption and divert entrepreneurial energy and resources from wealth-generating activity – diversions an aging society can ill afford. Where power and privilege get around market forces, the signal to others is that relationships matter more than competitiveness. When property rights are not protected, the fruits of innovation are uncertain.

The transition from mobilization through central planning remains to be completed by getting the "software" right: by allowing market forces to determine prices, by protecting property rights, and by fostering the foundation of rules, norms, and transparency on which to build other changes.[5] The necessary reforms are interrelated, and several in particular will go some distance towards sustaining economic growth: changing the role of the state to encourage the productivity growth necessary to raise incomes, modernizing the financial sector to allow it to use capital more efficiently, fixing local government finances by diversifying their revenues and modernizing land markets to reduce local governments' controversial dependence on land sales, and, finally, managing the winners and losers from reform and responding to the growing debate about individual rights and the rule of law.

THE CHANGING ROLE OF GOVERNMENT IN THE ECONOMY

Three aspects of the role of government in the Chinese economy are particularly important in the restructuring that is necessary for the country's long-term growth potential: the taxing and spending powers of the central and local governments, which affect income distribution; the setting of key input prices, which subsidize goods producers at the expense of households; and the governance of state-owned enterprises (SOEs).[6]

Taxation and Public Spending

The nature of government taxation, spending, and transfers changed steadily over the period from 2001 to 2010, but the overall effect of these changes has been modest. Agricultural taxes and the taxation of interest income were abolished in 2007, and personal tax exemptions were raised. These changes are estimated to have raised household disposable income by 1 per cent of GDP above what it otherwise would have been. Cuts to social insurance fund contribution rates have also helped.

Fourfold increases in direct spending on education, health, and social security over the 2002–10 period have had a more robust effect. Spending has expanded on the social safety net for urban residents, and a number of other initiatives – including a rural cooperative medical insurance program, rural pensions, and the elimination of tuition and school fees for 150 million primary school students – have begun to reduce direct costs for rural Chinese. Transfer payments to low-income urban households have begun, with rural programs to follow.

But there is much more to be done. For example, it is estimated that the freeing of interest rates paid on savings could raise private consumption as a share of GDP by five percentage points.[7] Expanded basic retirement, medical, unemployment, and maternity benefits have improved the lot of urban households, but as many as half the total – usually individuals who are retired, self-employed, or employed in the informal sector – still lack health insurance. By 2009 40 per cent of health expenditures were still funded by individuals themselves – an improvement, but still twice the share in the Mao Zedong era.

The Role of Government in Setting Input Prices

China's cabinet, the State Council, and its top economic planning commission, the National Development Reform Commission, still set key input prices, including interest rates and energy prices. Pricing policies for gasoline and diesel fuel have been volatile. Before 2000 gasoline and diesel fuel prices had been allowed to move towards full-cost retail pricing; after 2004 these policies were partly reversed as the price of oil imports rose, fell, then rose again up to 2011. Goods manufacturers benefited from subsidized fuel, leaving refiners caught in-between as the government varied its practice of compensating for their shrinking margins. In 2013 the country's new leaders signalled their intention to resume moving towards full-cost pricing. Electricity pricing is also an issue. Grid companies, which deliver electricity to users, must pay generating companies, and until 2007 their prices were based on full-cost pricing. But the price of coal, which fuels most generators, then rose while electricity users' prices remained unchanged, causing the profits of generating companies to disappear, leading to shortages even as power users continued to benefit from below-market prices.

Government in Business

SOEs operate in industries where private firms face entry restrictions. Despite government ownership, many have become profitable – in 2010 their profits were estimated to be equivalent to 5 per cent of GDP[8] – and there is wide support for transferring some of these profits to social spending. A dividend policy was approved in 2007 that set a sliding scale by the size of the enterprise. Rates initially were phased in and set too low, but recently they have been raised and now apply to a broader range of enterprises.

Oversight of SOEs is the responsibility of the State-Owned Assets Supervision and Administration Commission (SASAC), which was created in 2003 by consolidating several ministries involved in industrial production and which collects dividends from the SOEs. The Commission, however, has resisted attempts to channel dividends to the Ministry of Finance to fund expanded social spending, instead using them, according to some reports, as an investment bank would do – participating in risky but lightly regulated shadow banking activities and setting up affiliates that make property investments.[9]

It is worth pausing here to understand the purpose of SASAC. In 2006 SASAC identified "strategically important" sectors and called for the SOEs in these industries to "grow into leading world businesses." Li Rongrong, then SASAC's chairman, stated that "[s]tate capital must play a leading role in these sectors, which are the vital arteries of the national economy and essential to national security."[10] The sectors he was referring to – where the state was to remain the sole or majority owner of enterprises – included defence, power generation and distribution, oil and petrochemicals, telecommunications, coal, aviation, and shipping. SOEs were also directed to become "heavyweights" in machinery, automobiles, information technology, construction, base metals and steel, and chemicals. Reform and restructuring were to be encouraged to enhance competitiveness; ownership was to be diversified through shareholding or attracting strategic investors, and the number of SOEs owned by the central government (of which there were 161 at the time) was to be reduced. Today the size and economic contribution of SOEs and state-invested firms are difficult to estimate because of a lack of reporting and the wide range of forms of ownership.[11] There are thought to be between 100 and 120 central government SOEs, many of them large conglomerates with numerous affiliates that are expected to carry out a range of economic and social functions. The smallest SOE presence seems to be in manufacturing, but they dominate the services sector. Overall, the total number of SOEs is estimated to have expanded dramatically as lower levels of government have set up new ones.[12]

SOEs are expected to carry out governments' strategic goals. SASAC has improved the competitiveness and efficiency of many, but financial performance is sometimes undermined by requirements to deliver public services and to charge regulated prices for their products. One-quarter lose money;[13] others, such as Sinopec, PetroChina, and China National Offshore Oil Corporation, the three petroleum SOEs, have affiliates listed on international stock exchanges and aim to become globally diversified players. Government ownership stakes in such companies as Lenovo and Haier are less prominent and they operate more independently in international markets, but they are favoured companies with political and personal ties at home. Favoured companies are also seen to advance the ambitions of local governments to promote local champions, where competitiveness is less important than employment. In the steel industry, for example, the central government has a vision of a few large and highly competitive producers supplying local and international markets, but the industry remains fragmented as each province promotes its own local champion.[14]

Favoured firms are often kept alive by government's directing local banks to roll over loans or even cancel them to prevent bankruptcy, instead of requiring them to clean up their balance sheets and encouraging consolidation. Resources then are trapped in these "zombie" firms instead of being reallocated to more dynamic industries and firms. Zombies are especially prevalent in the real estate and financial sectors, where they are highly leveraged with high fixed costs. When economic growth slows, they get into trouble; if they are listed on stock markets, their performance pulls down the index.[15]

Other cases can be found in rapidly expanding industries such as solar power. For example, when a maker of solar modules first located in a city in Jiangxi province, the local government enthused about becoming a "silicon city," raised capital for it, and extended it favourable land and electricity prices. When growth slowed and the industry experienced overcapacity, the company fell behind on its bank debts. The local government then protected the company's creditors while seeking a potential purchaser from among other local companies, including SOEs not in the solar power industry, and incorporated a portion of the company's outstanding loans into its annual budget. The China Development Bank led talks between the bank's creditors and the local government and provided more loans – in large part because the local government was expected to make good. At the same time the company laid off thousands of employees and left many suppliers unpaid.[16]

According to the principles of market reform, the appropriate role of government is to provide public goods and services "the production of which result in unremunerated positive externalities" such as defence, infrastructure, social protection, and basic R&D.[17] If SASAC's mandate were revised accordingly, it would become the regulator and supervisor, rather than the owner, of SOEs. Government's scope for producing public goods remains significant, but this should be limited to social projects such as public housing and providing reliable electricity supplies and communications channels. Modern corporate practices would remove Party members from senior management appointments, accounting, and external audit. SASAC's ownership stakes would be transferred to professional state asset management companies subject to stringent rules of transparency. They would represent government interests, but transfer dividend payments to the treasury and gradually diversify their sectoral portfolios over time.[18]

SOEs are one part of the economy in which changes are being debated, but where there is likely to be significant pushback from these large, profitable, and politically favoured entities. SASAC, however, might be less likely to escape pressures to channel dividend income to support rebalancing since acquiescence might be a shrewd compromise that ensures its continued power.

MODERNIZING THE FINANCIAL SYSTEM

Another focus of reform to enable China to sustain long-term economic growth is the financial sector. Here, too, the state plays a prominent role through ownership and price setting. Government owns most commercial banks, sets interest rates, and manages the exchange rate. These policies, while understandable in the developmental context, are increasingly costly because of the distortions they create.

The Banking System

Household savers receive low returns on their bank deposits and, in the absence of efficient bond and equity markets, have few other available savings vehicles beyond investing in housing. At the same time, directed lending – such as that used to mitigate the effects of the 2008 financial crisis – supplements stimulus spending but adds to the banks' stocks of bad loans. Reports by the China Banking Regulatory Commission of non-performing loans, however, show a significant decline, from 39 per cent of GDP in 2002 to a modest 1.2 per cent in 2010. When impaired loans still on the books of asset management companies and the Ministry of Finance are included, however, the ratio climbs to 7-to-10 per cent of GDP.[19] Moreover, such numbers do not reflect the existing practice of rolling over or forgiving troubled loans.

Modernizing the financial system has been a work-in-progress for much of the reform period. The speed of change accelerated after China's accession to the World Trade Organization in 2001, when it negotiated a five-year window for its banks to learn to compete with those of foreign countries. Large stocks of legacy non-performing loans were moved from their books to those of state-financed asset management corporations charged with collecting or calling the loans. Four of China's largest banks were listed on stock exchanges and attracted strategic investments by foreign banks. All of these steps were designed to change the incentive frameworks of bank boards and managers to be more responsive to market forces and more transparent to market monitoring.

Much remains to be done, however, as measured by the role of the financial system in supporting growth in wide sectors of the economy. Deposit rates have risen somewhat, but they are still regulated. Chinese banks have become accustomed to riskless income from the generous spread between deposit and lending rates, and many lack the expertise needed to manage risk.

SME Finance and Shadow Banking

This risk aversion, whereby bank managers have few incentives to take on risky, unknown, and unconnected customers and which was well known even before the global financial crisis, makes it difficult for the small and medium enterprises (SMEs) that create most of China's new jobs, to access formal finance. For their part, SMES are suspicious of the strings attached to formal lending, preferring loans from family, friends, or informal unregulated underground lenders who charge interest rates that are as high as 22 per cent.

In the wake of the 2011–12 growth slowdown, the dearth of formal funding became a policy issue, particularly in the coastal city of Wenzhou in Zhejiang province, known for its aggressive and ambitious entrepreneurs, most of whom are owners of SMEs. In the past decade as many as 400,000 firms in Wenzhou have taken part in RMB 110 billion in underground lending and borrowing.[20] Wenzhou's entrepreneurs were hit hard by tighter credit conditions imposed on state-owned banks in 2011 and by a credit crackdown on shadow banks and informal lenders. Many saw their businesses go bankrupt, some fled to avoid their debts, and still others even committed suicide.

Shadow banking is a recent development that includes a number of off-balance-sheet transactions between the banks and unregulated non-bank financial institutions such as trust companies. The banks raise large amounts of cash from wealthy customers by offering short-term, high-return wealth management products via the trust companies, thereby keeping the transaction off the banks' books. The cash is then lent onward through the trust companies to such risky borrowers as property developers, local government financing vehicles, and SMEs at substantially higher interest rates, also off the banks' books. The magnitude of these activities in 2012 was, by various estimates, between 46.5 and 69 per cent of annual GDP.[21] Borrowers' high risk profiles contribute to growing uncertainty as to who will bear the losses in the event of default as the economy slows and restructures.

These activities have complicated significantly both the conduct of monetary policy and the regulation of financial institutions. While the central bank is carefully managing monetary tightening financial regulators are experimenting with ways to bring such activity into the regulatory net. At the same time regulators are experimenting with ways to supply more formal finance to SMEs. An initiative in Wenzhou that began in 2012 includes plans to give lending companies direct access to overseas investment and to establish professional asset management firms. First steps included setting up a registration centre, permitting banks to issue special bonds earmarked for small business lending, to assign lower risk weights to such loans, and to tolerate higher default rates.[22]

Capital Markets

China's underdeveloped capital markets are another focus of reform, and a number of small steps taken in 2012 will help to strengthen them and make them more open and contestable. The China Securities Regulatory Commission (CSRC) has moved to strengthen the Shanghai and Shenzhen stock markets. It has also eased restrictions on foreigners who operate in China, who engage in RMB transactions under the Qualified Foreign Institutional Investor program, and who trade in the domestic interbank market, where most fixed-income trading occurs. Future reforms under discussion include permitting short selling and launching institutional margin financing to enhance market depth and boost hedge fund operations.[23]

Most corporate bonds are issued by state enterprises, but a non-state enterprise bond market is in its early stages, with much of the activity taking place in the fixed-income departments of banks. As recently as 2007 the value of enterprise and corporate bonds was less than one-tenth the value of government and financial bonds.[24] The CSRC itself recommends speeding up bond market development with a number of changes that indicate the distance still to be travelled in creating a deep and sound market. The list begins with a unified regulatory framework to replace the present splintered authorities, and calls for clear approval procedures, disclosure rules for bond issuers, an improved credit-rating system, clearer and enforced penalties for violators, buyer education, an interconnected trading and settlements system, and encouragement of product innovation.[25] All of these changes will move things in the right direction, but a change of particular significance is interest-rate deregulation because of its direct positive effects on household income and the impact of higher deposit rates on lending rates, which will increase the cost of capital for capital-intensive goods manufacturers.[26] Flexible interest rates will also require a flexible exchange rate, which, as it appreciates, will raise costs for goods exporters and reduce import prices for everyone else.

More work is also required to strengthen the foundations necessary for more efficient use of capital. A diverse, transparent, efficient, and rules-based financial system is an essential building block in a complex industrial economy, particularly with respect to auditing and accounting standards, in which investors and issuers must have confidence if bond and equity markets are to function soundly. Without sound and liquid capital markets and an efficient, well-run banking sector, China would be ill advised to open its still-restricted capital account. Yet until the capital account is open fully, the international role of China's currency, the renminbi, likely will be restricted to regional trade partners, as we will see in Chapter 4. In the Twelfth Five-Year Plan, financial officials set quantitative targets for 2015, but the Plan is silent on institutional changes that would allow market forces freely to determine interest and exchange rates, make the capital account fully convertible, and reduce the state's ownership of banks.

LAND RIGHTS AND LOCAL GOVERNMENT FINANCES

A third area of reform in the interest of long-term economic growth concerns local governments, which rely mainly on land conversion to finance the services they are expected to deliver. Their finances are frequently characterized as "a mess." Transactions often take place on an extra-budgetary basis and, lacking a tax base or the financial instruments to raise revenues, their main budgetary source is land sales. Since the establishment of the People's Republic in 1949, all land has belonged to the people. Rural land is owned by village collectives and leased out to farming households, which receive thirty-year contractual rights. With urbanization, however, more and more of the land surrounding towns and cities has been acquired from farmers and sold to real estate developers and builders of transportation and other infrastructure. Failure to protect farmers' interests in the process has led to hundreds of thousands of disputes, often violent. The common practice has been to requisition land and offer farmers compensation based on the going price for agricultural land, then sell it to developers at much higher urban land prices and pocket the difference. Such a practice effectively taxes farmers at a rate of 100 per cent on capital gains and provides abundant opportunities for corruption. Lack of consultation and legal recourse add to the sense of unfairness. The central authorities are well aware of the contradictions between the services local governments are expected to provide and their limited revenue sources, just as they are aware of the problems of land reform. In 2012, some local governments were permitted to tap bond markets, but land sales continue to predominate.

On the other side, farmers need more options. Because they do not own their land, they are unable to use it as collateral or to sell it – although they are permitted to lease out their contractual rights. There should be channels to realize the land's value when landholders depart for city jobs, leaving their land lying fallow; such flexibility would increase the efficiency with which land is used, and it would raise rural incomes, but no such reform has yet been undertaken. Outright privatization is a logical option, but is largely rejected for fear that it would open the door to ruthless consolidation of rural lands and exploitation of the farmers.

The intermediate route is to find more flexible market-oriented procedures that would prevent such outcomes. Experiments with *hukou* reform in Chongqing municipality have revealed some avenues for flexibility. There, land-trading systems have set up exchanges through which farmers can search on their own for buyers and negotiate the transfer price. Groups of farmers have been persuaded to give up their plots in exchange for new housing in nearby cities or villages. These plots are then consolidated and the land returned to agriculture, this time with some scale economies. The local government is then entitled to sell an equivalent amount of land for urban development. In more distant areas, land can be traded through the *dipiao* land trading system, whereby farmers exchange their plots for village housing, earning local governments a credit, or *dipiao*, which they can then auction on a rural property exchange. The buyer acquires the right to develop an equivalent amount of land on the city outskirts, with the sale proceeds distributed to the village collective and the original farmers.

A similar scheme is used in Chengdu prefecture in Sichuan province, where the devastation caused by the 2008 earthquake was a catalyst. Villages built since the earthquake have been populated by newly homeless farmers previously scattered throughout the surrounding countryside who have been persuaded to give up their land use rights to the village collective in exchange for a modern house with water, electricity, and sewage services and a small plot nearby on which to grow vegetables. The village collective then commits to farm the land consolidated in this way – in 2011 the author visited a village in a hilly area where kiwi fruit (or Chinese gooseberry) was the chosen cash crop – and trades the right with a collective nearer to Chengdu that then "sells" the rights to urban developers who acquire an equivalent amount of rural land for development in the Chengdu suburbs. The rural collective then decides what to do with the funds earned in this way; in the wake of the earthquake, such funds have financed the rural reconstruction and provision of the modern services – including social centres, restaurants, and mini-marts – available in the new villages.[27]

Land reform will remain closely connected with local government finance until local governments have more financial options. Premier Li Keqiang's proposal for municipal bonds lacks the necessary capital market infrastructure, however, and farmers are unlikely to be allowed to sell their land outright any time soon. Another proposal is to reform the vetting process for the transfer of rural land to urban use, and with it the compensation process, which would see land valued at market prices and the value passed through to farmers, who would then pay a capital gains tax (but less than the existing 100 per cent). In this way local governments would acquire a transparent flow of income that, over time, should be complemented by a system of property taxation, both of which would provide a more sustainable revenue base.[28]

WHY THE NEXT STAGE IS SO DIFFICULT

The preceding analysis paints a picture of China's partial reform and restructuring in the face of the rising costs of its unbalanced growth. On the supply side further market reforms will depend on recognizing property and individual rights and on building a foundation of rules, norms, and transparency. Public spending to rebalance demand has increased and household taxation has been eased, but the social safety net needed to reduce precautionary saving still has to be financed.

The necessary reforms will create winners and losers. Potential losers with political power will resist change, and powerful groups with privilege and strong vested interests are pushing back. Significantly, however, the less powerful know what they are missing, as the Internet and social networks showcase growing income inequality, the weakness of the social safety net, and the wealth amassed by those with privilege and connections. They are pushing forward. The new leadership team has signalled its commitment to cleaning up corruption and speeding up reforms, but its primary focus continues to be the growth and jobs essential to Party legitimacy. Its challenge is to find modern versions of the political successes of the early 1980s in which potential opponents also benefited from economic reforms.

China has many dramatic stories of entrepreneurs who started with nothing but a few yuan from parents or friends and through hard work and shrewd investments built fortunes by filling niches or starting entire new industries. At the same time, stories of crony capitalism abound on the Internet and in social media – of the acquisition by Party members and relatives of officials of fortunes that could not possibly be the result of hard work or shrewd investment, but of the corrupt exercise of privilege, the use of insider knowledge, and the earning of grey income though participation in asset bubbles and tax evasion.[29]

Rent seeking occurs when the state monopolizes the allocation of property rights through its laws, regulations, subsidies, taxes, and procurement practices. State intervention creates more monopolies. In these situations, players whose options are thus restricted will try to influence state allocations in their favour, allowing the state to affect both the supply of and demand for preferential treatment. Although such competition can be legal, it often takes the form of bribes, corruption, and smuggling. The black market for foreign exchange, ubiquitous on the streetcorners of cities and towns in countries with fixed exchange rates, is a well-known example. Another example is family behaviour motivated by job seeking, when favouritism and political connections matter more than a candidate's achievements; it can even mean moving to the capital city to cultivate connections or to bribe officials who have the power to award jobs.

In authoritarian China, social protest, rather than legal or political action, is the traditional channel for righting wrongs. Social demonstrations have been increasing since the 1990s and now are thought to occur between one hundred thousand and two hundred thousand times a year – a protest every three minutes! Some protests are effective. In rural areas ordinary people have taken on corrupt and capricious local officials and worked to shut down illegal activities such as mining and quarrying or to prevent the seizure of farm land. They have also sought to ensure that village-level elections allow non-Party officials to contest, exposing, with the help of civil society and journalists, the rigging of elections by official attempting bribery.[30] In urban areas, too, households occasionally have blocked unwanted infrastructure and industrial projects.

Increasingly, however, the Party uses a classic carrot-and-stick approach to protests. The stick is police action; the carrot is the practice of compensating the noisiest protestors, such as farmers and householders seeking adequate compensation for expropriated property. If troublemakers persist with litigation, however, judges reportedly are told to mediate the differences rather than to adjudicate them. A budget for financial compensation – *weiwen*, or stability maintenance – is now included in spending on law and order approved annually by the National People's Congress; significantly, in 2011 this budget exceeded military spending.[31] Instead of removing the causes, however, *weiwen* encourages more protests.

The common thread that runs through this story of corruption and protest is uncertainty about where the goalposts are, given the lack of transparent rules and laws. "Socialism with Chinese characteristics" provided the rationale for the Party's maintaining tight political control during the early period of reform and opening up to the outside world. Now, the expanding middle classes, who support China's auto market, now the world's largest, who travel in high-speed trains, and who increasingly even wish to fly in their own planes, are exercising consumer and investor choice. Why would they not also want more choice about new ventures and more say in how their taxes are spent, demand greater accountability from their rulers, and insist on equal treatment under the law? Younger Chinese, born since the Cultural Revolution and the Tiananmen Square tragedy, have grown up with the Internet and do not appreciate the Party's arbitrary restrictions.

The Rule of Law or Rule by Law?

China has a comprehensive legal framework, but the Party continues to believe it knows best. Wu Bangguo, former leader of the Standing Committee of the National People's Congress, referred in 2011 to "a socialist legal system with Chinese characteristics," one that is a "complete set of laws covering all areas of social relations."[32]

What kind of legal system actually exists in China? In countries where governance proceeds from the rule of law, the separation of the state and the legal system is intended to checks abuses of state power. Ideally, laws are clearly written and well understood, leaving no opportunities or incentives to engage in rent seeking and legal violations. The judicial system is strong, capable, and transparent, and the independent judiciary is free from interference from administrative and political officials.

China's legal system differs from Western views of democracy and the rule of law for good reasons, some argue. The Western paradigm views government as responsible to the people; the Chinese paradigm, in contrast, sees government as responsible *for* the people. Chinese history is replete with examples that offer an explanation for how Chinese tend to think about the rule of law today. Confucianism tied the legitimacy of rulers to their duties to the people. Mencius, one of Confucius's' disciples, justified the removal of rulers who failed adequately to serve the people; another, Shin Za, emphasized the importance of equitable and clear law applied evenly to all – but with the key exception of the ruler.[33]

With the coming of the 1949 Revolution, Mao Zedong established a dictatorial "rule of man" and undertook costly experiments involving class struggle. This era was largely overturned by Deng Xiaoping, and since 1982 China has had both national and Party constitutions that affirm government by law, the superiority of law, and equality before the law. The Party has filled the legal vacuum with a criminal code, civil law, and contract law. It created a Ministry of Justice, reopened law schools that had been closed, and professionalized judges, procurators, lawyers, and police officers. Within this structure, citizens have become increasingly able and willing to challenge the state.[34]

How is the system performing? In the absence of enforceable contracts and with limited checks on abuses of power, people continue to rely on trust-based relationships through informal social networks called *guanxi*. Abuse of power and disregard for the law is hardly unknown among those at the highest levels – the case of Bo Xilai, former secretary of the Chongqing Committee of the Communist Party of China, is a notorious one. At lower levels many people consider themselves above the law: examples readily can be found on China's crowded highways and city ring roads, where SUVs with tinted windows and licence plates obscured from public view move aggressively through congested traffic lanes. Should they collide with another driver they leave the accident scene. Friends of mine travelling in southern China recount an incident where an SUV with People's Liberation Army plates circumvented stalled traffic on a highway crowded with weekend travellers by driving on the outside shoulder. When the SUV accidentally sideswiped the vehicle driven by my friends, the driver stopped and agreed that the police and the insurance firm should be called. After interviewing the guilty party, the police officer said to my friends, "Are you sure you want to pursue this complaint? This driver is a gangster you don't want to tangle with." My friends decided to settle with the insurance firm and not to pursue the matter.

Chinese elites appear not to believe they are subject to the same rules as the general population. A "Party state" exists alongside the legal state that applies to everyone else, repression is used to prevent local protests from spreading, and petitioners who persist in taking their grievances to Beijing in time-worn fashion frequently are punished and incarcerated by local authorities and their agents in Beijing, all of which causes growing cynicism about justice and fairness. A US legal expert notes how the growth of legal education and research in China has become an increasing factor in activists' and citizens' demands for justice, to such an extent that the Party perceives them as a threat to its monopoly. Since the 2007 Party Congress the leadership has pushed back to maintain its domination of the legal system, using the public security apparatus in what has been called an evolving "people's warfare."[35]

As more Chinese accumulate wealth, concerns have grown about the risks of uncertain property rights and social disorder, causing many to send their children abroad for education, to move their financial assets offshore, and even to move abroad themselves.[36] It has been estimated that customers of one of the largest banks held assets abroad equivalent to 3 per cent of China's GDP in 2011, and even the somewhat less wealthy, those with investable assets of RMB 3–6 million, are beginning to move assets abroad in the search for security and privacy.[37] Rather than punitive action, the appropriate government response to such fears would be to protect property rights and allow greater diversity of investment options. Yet, as a report in the *Economist* magazine has noted, the government continues to rely on punishment: 17 per cent of the wealthiest Chinese entrepreneurs were investigated, charged, or arrested over a particular period compared with 7 per cent of other entrepreneurs.[38]

Is the legal system evolving in ways that address these weaknesses? Areas of particular concern are the relationship of the Party to the legal system and the lack of judicial independence. This relationship is apparent even from the name of the top judicial institution: the Central Commission of Politics and Law (CCPL) of the Central Committee of the Communist Party of China. The CCPL is thus an organ of the Party, which operates at every level of society and has a police force to enforce its decisions. Cases are heard by judges, but judgments on sensitive cases are vetted politically before being rendered at court, and judges are subject to disciplinary action for their decisions. In top-down fashion, the head of the CCPL traditionally was a member of the Politburo Standing Committee, drawn from career Party and police officials. Until the Eighteenth Party Congress in November 2012, the incumbent had no legal training. His successor is a former minister of public security and former provincial Party chief. More positively, the position was dropped from the seven-member Politburo Standing Committee, possibly signalling the Party's support of the rule of law and a move to reduce the power of the CCPL – although it might have been a rebuke for the CCPL's handling of the Bo Xilai affair. The appointment of Zhou Qiang – widely respected for his work on the application of rule of law in Hunan province – as president of the Supreme Court is also a positive development.[39]

In discussions about how the CCPL should be supervised, it has been suggested that this role by taken on by the Party's Discipline Inspection Commission, by the CCPL's own internal disciplinary body, or by the member of the Politburo Standing Committee who is responsible for the National People's Congress, to which the courts, procurators, judges, and police report. The answers are interrelated. An incremental step to increase judicial independence would be to place judges, police, and prosecutors on a level playing field – at present the police run the show because of their higher political rank. Another step would be to remove the courts from the political jurisdiction of the CCPL, leaving it in control of state and public security and the justice ministry.[40] Such steps would be in the right direction, but a long way from a system of judicial independence.

Who, then, rules? Clearly, rule by law still characterizes the system, but with exceptions in trade, investment, and intellectual property, where legal frameworks apply – although they are not always enforced. Some legal experts emphasize how far the Chinese economy has progressed even without the rule of law or enforceable property rights, but these deficiencies have deterred foreign investment and inhibited reform of SOEs.[41] Leading legal scholars are also debating changes in the system. He Weifang, Peking University law professor and well-known reform activist, has campaigned tirelessly for an independent judiciary and the reorganization of the legal system to act as a check on power, rather than as complicit in the exercise of power. He argues that China's race is between a bottom-up revolution and judicial reform, and that the Party should comply with the both the national and Party constitutions to regulate party affairs and the behaviour of its members.[42] Yu Keping, respected Party member and academic, also believes the Party must exercise its power within the dictates of the country's and the Party's constitutions. He advocates a road map beginning with experiments with democratization, arguing that, as long as officials lack incentives to experiment, there will be institutional inertia. The road map should be designed to minimize risks and costs, and it should rely more on negotiation and less on repression. It should be incremental, beginning with experiments at the grassroots and within the Party – including intra-Party elections and oversight systems for decisions and policy making – and new mechanisms for consultation, such as public hearings, opinion surveys, petitions, and the permitting of group protests.[43]

Whether China's leaders intend anything more than incremental change is a question raised by the inconclusive saga of a land dispute at Wukan, a village in south China where Party officials appropriated common cultivated land for development and attacked and jailed protestors. The violence was videotaped and scenes posted on the Internet, making the protests an international sensation. With some high-level intervention, villagers were permitted to elect new leaders, but there was no follow-on intervention to assist them in reclaiming their land. Instead, villagers encountered murky details of ownership and political involvement in the transactions. According to one authoritative account, contract law invalidates land-transfer agreements if the contract was obtained by fraudulent or coercive means, but the ambiguous status of the disputed land has complicated decisions to return it. Two years on, the case remains in limbo.[44]

It appears the jury is still out on these politically sensitive questions. The risks of transitioning to a system with freer play of market forces, greater legal and regulatory transparency, lighter political control, and more openness appear still to outweigh the perceived risks of moving forward, however slowly. Unless there is a crisis.

REFORM OR CRISIS?

China is at a turning point. Market forces are operating relatively freely in product markets, but the state continues to control most of the factors of production and monopolizes key industries. Without reforms, distortions will continue to undermine China's long-term growth potential, and diminishing returns are likely to result as energies are diverted to rent seeking from wealth creation and innovation.

At the same time, China's growing middle classes are weighing the evidence of corruption and privilege against growing income inequality, and are pushing for political change, greater trans-parency, and checks on abuses of power. Punishing miscreants, however, merely changes the cost-benefit calculus, rather than eliminating the drawbacks of the Party state. It is far from clear that the state is prepared to loosen its grip and take the contro-versial and politically difficult step of confining itself to produc-ing public goods and setting the framework for the private sector. Freer play of market forces in allocating land, labour, and capital would serve the imperative of relying less on mobilization and more on productivity growth. Significantly greater emphasis on ownership rights is needed, fundamentally through reform of the legal system, but also by the adoption of a modern capital markets infrastructure of transparent rules, strong audit standards, and ac-ceptable accounting rules.

A Viable Action Plan? Signals from the Top

Finding a politically and economically viable action plan for car-rying forward essential elements of reform will preoccupy China's leaders for the foreseeable future. Some early and general indica-tions of the way ahead were issued by the State Council in May 2013, and could be a foreshadow of the economic agenda at the Party's October 2013 meeting. The list includes stepping back from rules setting and regulation, financial modernization, action on energy and resources pricing, urbanization and rural issues, some privatization, and attention to technological innovation.[45] But other important dimensions of an action plan could cascade through the system, including the commitment on the part of the leadership to greater transparency and more open accountability and willingness to create opportunities to roll back even further the state's monopoly powers, particularly on property rights.

Set the Tone
China's leaders could send a powerful public signal by cutting back on privileges. In early 2013 Xi Jinping built on his rhetorical

pledge to curb official excesses and tackle corruption by publicly calling on officials to end extravagant gifts and parties during the spring festival. An example of this kind of message occurred in the Philippines, where President Benigno Aquino III announced in his June 2010 inaugural address new rules curbing the ways elites use their power: "No more junkets, no more senseless spending. No more turning back on pledges made during the campaign ... no more stealing. No more sirens, no more short cuts, no more bribes. It is time for us to work together once more."[46] The reference to sirens was his banning their use in Manila's dense traffic, including for his own motorcade, except by fire engines and ambulances. The populace was duly impressed by this simple but highly visible curbing of elite power. Anyone whose travelling around a major Chinese city has been impeded by unexplained and lengthy closures of major thoroughfares, presumably while motorcades of black SUVs of senior officials are on the move, understands how such behaviour infuriates ordinary citizens.

Make Disclosure of Personal Assets Mandatory
The sensitive issue of the accumulation of personal wealth by Party and government officials was the subject of public discussion around disclosures in Western newspapers in 2012 of the riches allegedly amassed by the families of Premier Wen Jiabao, President Xi Jinping, and the disgraced Bo Xilai. The appointment of Wang Qishan to head the Central Commission for Discipline Inspection sent a strong message that the Party leadership meant business – at least after the fact. Regulations requiring officials to report personal assets already had been adopted in 2006, but never enforced. Is this latest initiative "loud thunder but small raindrops," in the Chinese turn of phrase? To implement the rules, real-name registration will have to become mandatory in banking, real estate, and elsewhere.[47]

Design and Disclose a Reform Road Map and Accompanying Mileposts
A further signal that the leadership means business would be to approve, possibly at the October 2013 Party conference, a public reform road map with mileposts and public accountability. The

road map could be developed in consultation with a reform commission supported by the highest levels of government, something suggested in *China 2030*, the joint study by the World Bank and the Development Research Center of the State Council. Public accountability would help to deal with those most likely to oppose reforms because they stand to lose power and benefits. Such an approach would also help take on potential losers from industrial change and opinion leaders who believe the problems are caused by earlier reforms rather than by distortions of the current hybrid system.[48] The road to reform should start with highly popular programs such as building a social safety net, increasing investment in human capital, and creating opportunities for public participation in the reform process. Moves should also be made to increase SOE dividends and channel them into the treasury, levy market prices for industrial inputs, and impose transparent taxation of capital gains.[49] Halting forced land conversions would be more difficult as it would require the cooperation of local governments.

Remove State Monopolies and Enforce Property Rights
Since government rules and monopolies restrict economic activity and create opportunities for rent seeking behaviour, curtailing them could enhance China's economic potential. Since 2003 the International Finance Corporation and the World Bank have published an annual index of the ease of doing business in nearly two hundred countries. Countries with the highest rankings are those in which the rules are simple and designed to make markets work better; the more rules the more corruption and the smaller the tax base. Simplifying the rules would release economic potential and cost the economy nothing.[50] Easiest to implement would be the removal of restrictions on interest rates and the exchange rate, since these are entirely within the central government's mandate. Besides the direct benefits to consumers, such changes, along with capital account liberalization, would force greater competition in the banking sector, increase the efficiency of capital allocation, and release the central bank from intervening in the foreign-exchange market.

Choose Opportunities for Experimentation and Competition
The Twelfth Five-Year Plan opens a window of opportunity to reduce SOE monopolies by aiming to promote seven emerging industries: a "new-energy auto industry"; energy conservation and
environmental protection; renewable energy; new information
technology, such as networks, advanced electronics, and software;
biotechnology; high-end equipment manufacturing, including
aviation, satellites, and high-speed trains; and new materials. Monopoly interests have not yet vested in these industries, so participation could be opened to any firm wishing to invest in them,
regardless of ownership. If there is one area of the economy
where consensus might be found for new ways of doing things,
it is in industries that will thrive only with innovation, new ideas,
and capital.

New ideas and initiatives are more likely to succeed, however,
when intellectual property rights are protected, but rather than
changing the incentive structure, China seems to want to achieve
its technological ambitions by large amounts of public spending.
The spectacular crash of a high-speed train and resulting loss of
life in July 2011 is a graphic illustration of the corruption and
cutting of corners at all levels of the value chain in response to
overambitious goals.[51]

Another window for experimentation exists in the financial sector. Instead of top-down decrees from the central bank, bottom-
up innovations are providing modern services and transactions.
Ten cities, including Wenzhou, Shenzhen, Tianjin, and Chang-
sha, are experimenting with modern financial services, facilitating
cross-border financial flows, and the support of city clusters, rural
finance, and securities transactions.[52]

Innovation in institutions, not just in products and processes,
should be the hallmark of experimentation. Can China create
new knowledge, or is it condemned by its institutions with Chinese characteristics to rely on the knowledge created by others?
Examples of adaptation of existing technologies abound – some
industries, such as heavy equipment, are moving to the technology frontier. But the increasingly fraught issue of intellectual prop-

erty theft raises questions about the state's willingness to change incentives to encourage innovation – indeed, organized theft is widely alleged in US media to be sanctioned by the state. An example is a 2013 report of cyber espionage supposedly conducted by a unit of the People's Liberation Army.[53] This was followed closely by a Pentagon report on China to the US Congress that used strong terms to describe China's cyber espionage, prompting charges that China is an "all-in enterprise with every resource of the state employed to plunder US technology" for defence and civilian purposes.[54]

The possibility that China is in a countdown to a crisis cannot be discounted. Its leaders appeared to recognize this when they introduced bold proposals in May 2013 to roll back government regulation and permit private ownership in finance, energy, railways, and parts of telecommunications. Restrictions on foreign investment in finance, logistics, and health care services are also to be eased.[55] These are first steps, but a stronger verdict on change must await future Party Congress meetings. Meanwhile, informed netizens and citizens with rising expectations of a better deal support a faster pace of restructuring. More action is needed to free up capital for risky innovative enterprises, many of them small but crucial to future job creation. Deeper institutional reforms are required to curb privilege and abuse of power at the top, to subject all equally to the law, and to reduce government's grip on the economy, particularly in the services sector. The alternative is below-potential economic growth and rising disaffection with the Party's social compact with the population. High-level energetic commitment is needed. The Party drags its feet at its peril.

4 China's Growing International Footprint

China has an increasingly broad "footprint" across the globe, but it is not particularly deep.

– David Shambaugh[1]

China's unprecedented rise has seen its transformation from an inward-looking subsistence economy to one of the world's major destinations for investment and Asia's hub in global supply chains. Its increasing integration with the world economy has followed several major channels, with mixed implications. Some are positive. China is now the world's largest goods exporter, and the world's consumers have benefited from wider choice and lower prices. With the internationalization of the renminbi (RMB), the costs of trade with its major trading partners have declined. Increasingly, China is becoming a source of tourists, trade, and outward investment, the stock of which grew sixfold between 2005 and 2011, making it the world's twelfth-largest investor. With state encouragement China's enterprises are seeking in a range of industries to become national champions in international markets.

Other channels, however, are causing unease. China is now the world's largest emitter of greenhouse gases – a source of domestic concern as well. Its competition is growing with other countries, not least the United States and its increasingly assertive boundary and natural resources claims in offshore waters have alarmed its neighbours.

China's international footprint evokes ambivalence as well as welcome. We will all have to learn to live with a colossus that successfully manages its way through its formidable domestic challenges. If China stumbles, we will all feel the effects.

TRADE

Since China's economy was opened to the world in the 1980s and again following its accession to the World Trade Organization (WTO) in 2001, China's successful penetration of international markets for its consumer products has been an important factor in job growth. Chinese exports and imports, a mere 3 per cent of global totals in 2000, exploded to 8 per cent of global totals by 2011 (Figure 4.1). Data from both the US Department of Commerce and China's Custom Administration agree that the dollar value of China's goods trade (at US$3.87 trillion) surpassed that of the United States (at US$3.82 trillion) in 2012[2] – although adding services trade would bring the US total to US$4.9 trillion. China's soaring goods trade reflects its openness to foreign investment, the domestic benefits of undervaluing the RMB/US dollar exchange rate, and, more recently, China's growing importance as an importer in global supply chains.

These measures, however, are all based on final goods. The story changes significantly when the measure is the value added by the Chinese production process. A well-known example is Apple's iPod: the final good shows up as a Chinese export, but the Chinese contribution to its manufacture – namely, assembling the product – is only ten per cent of its total value. Recent efforts by international organizations such as the WTO to measure value added thus cast a new light on trade balances within global supply chains. If the large US-Chinese trade deficit were recalculated on the basis of value added, it would be 25 per cent smaller – in effect, the United States is actually importing components sourced from the multiple suppliers of China's assemblers.[3]

Yet China's manufacturing capabilities are also moving towards the technological frontier. China is the key location for the assembly and export of final products in a wide range of technologically

Figure 4.1. Exports and Imports, China and United States, as Shares of Global Trade, 2000–11

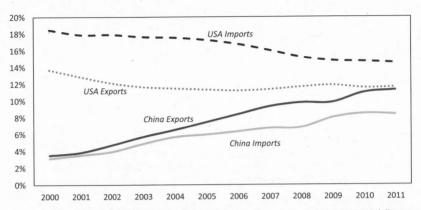

Notes: Exports and imports include both goods and services. Data are in constant 2000 US dollars.
Source: http://databank.worldbank.org/ddp/home.do

sophisticated consumer products like the iPod. In industries such as autos, construction equipment, and machine tools, intense domestic competition and economies of scale are encouraging the development of local capabilities sufficient to achieve product quality that meets international standards. Not only are these Chinese manufacturers competing successfully with foreign producers in the domestic market, they are increasingly able to venture abroad.[4]

More recently China has joined its Asian neighbours in negotiating regional trade agreements. Such agreements have a strong foreign policy motivation: to demonstrate China's friendly intentions. The headline trade agreement is with the Association of Southeast Asian Nations (ASEAN), signed in 2005. South Korea (2006), Japan (2008), and India (2010) then followed suit with their own agreements with ASEAN. In all, China is now studying or has concluded twenty-seven regional or bilateral agreements,[5] mostly with other countries in Asia, although one has also been completed with a developed economy, New Zealand, in part because of the highly complementary goods trade between the two

Figure 4.2. Outward Stocks of Direct Foreign Investment: China, Hong Kong, Japan, and United States, 2000–11 (US$ trillions)

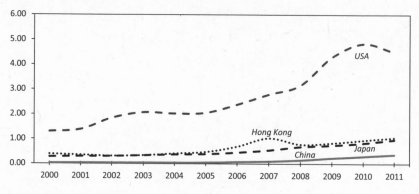

Source: UNCTAD, *World Investment Report*, various years.

countries. Australia and China, however, have been negotiating unsuccessfully for eight years because of differences over their treatment of direct investment and issues around the movement of people.

CHINESE INVESTMENT ABROAD

Starting from a very low level a decade ago, Chinese capital is now flowing abroad in increasingly large amounts (Figure 4.2). The United Nations Conference on Trade and Development (UNCTAD), the repository of official global statistics on direct investments and mergers and acquisitions, ranked China in the top dozen largest outward investors in 2011 with a total stock of US$366 billion, representing 1.7 per cent of global stocks held abroad, though still below US (US$4.5 trillion, or 21.3 per cent), Japanese (US$963 billion, or 4.5 per cent), and even Canadian (US$670 billion, 3.2 per cent) stocks.[6] Still, if China were to follow a trajectory similar to Japan's at the same stage of its development, it is estimated that more than a trillion dollars could flow out of China in the next decade – a veritable tidal wave that would change the face of business sectors in many countries.[7]

Already, however, the investments of Chinese businesses abroad are a source of unease, particularly given the enthusiasm with which they are acquiring assets in countries such as the United States. Chinese enterprises that wish to invest abroad do so with the advantage of active Chinese government policy encouragement and support to "go out," as a result of the decision in 2006 to build state-owned enterprises (SOEs) into national champions, a policy that now includes non-state-owned enterprises as well. They are encouraged, moreover, to access the natural resources required to feed China's industries, as well as to enter new markets, acquire brands, and foreign technology. As well, the global economic downturn since 2008 has created unique opportunities for Chinese firms to scoop up distressed assets at reasonable prices. Chinese firms also have healthy balance sheets due to their oligopolistic positions in home markets, they pay minimal dividends to the state, and they benefit from subsidized prices of inputs such as energy, land, and environmental costs. There is also debate about their ability to access relatively cheaper capital through loans from large banks than can their international competitors, although the evidence appears to indicate that this is not the case.[8]

These enterprises, at the same time, face a number of disadvantages. They are inexperienced late comers, and many of the world's most desirable assets and locations have already been taken by experienced investors from more advanced economies. As well, although many SOEs are huge oligopolies or monopolies in the home market, with close ties to their government owners and regulators, they have little experience with international business practices and global rules of the road. Lack of such knowledge can erode the profitability of a transaction when inexperienced managers misinterpret or fail to take local business conditions and regulatory environments into account – although such risks are not unique to Chinese investors.

Of China's five largest leading outward non-financial investors, four appear in the *Fortune* Global 500 by market capitalization: Sinopec (number 5), China National Offshore Oil Corporation (CNOOC) (101), Lenovo (370), and Huawei (351), all of which are recognizable brands. The fifth, Haier, is not yet on the Global 500 list. These enterprises invest in energy, information technology and telecommunications hardware, and consumer white goods (kitchen appliances such as refrigerators and washing machines). It is estimated that, by 2010, 12,000 Chinese parent companies had invested in 34,000 affiliates abroad,[9] and that, in the first half of 2012 alone, 2,407 Chinese enterprises expanded their businesses in 117 countries with mergers and acquisitions worth US$30 billion.[10] Over the period between 2006 and 2009, SOEs accounted for an estimated 69 per cent of China's outflows. More recently privately owned enterprises have joined the fray, with Dalian Wanda's US$2.6 billion acquisition of AMC Entertainment Holdings, the world's second-largest theatre chain; Haier's US$700 million bid for Fisher & Paykel Appliances Holdings of New Zealand; and Wanxiang's US $26 million acquisition of the assets of US car battery maker A 123 Inc.[11] By industry, 77 per cent of these investment transactions were in the services industries – particularly in business services, finance, and trade – 18 per cent were in mining and petroleum, and only 5 per cent in manufacturing.[12] So far, much of this activity has been mergers and acquisitions, rather than "greenfield" investments in new capacity.

What are the prospects for the long-term success of these transactions? Host governments of advanced countries have a number of reservations about Chinese investors, some of which echo similar concerns about Japanese investors three decades ago. A major one is that SOEs are agents of the Chinese government and, as such, will make decisions based on political, rather than commercial, criteria, which could undermine the host country's national sovereignty. The concern is magnified by China's opaque political system and its 2006 decision to expand the role of SOEs in sectors considered critical to its own national and economic security. Another reservation is about Chinese investors' willingness to abide by host countries' regulatory regimes, a concern amplified by recent reports of cyber attacks on government and enterprise networks that have been traced back to the Chinese military. Still another concern relates to the perceived unfair advantages conferred on SOEs in their home market through the lack of a level playing field for non-state and foreign competitors.

A key concern is the opacity of SOE governance. The Chinese government, through the State-Owned Assets Supervision and Administration Commission (SASAC), owns the parent SOEs, and the Central Organization Department appoints and evaluates their chief executive officers (CEOs). Heads of the largest SOEs have ministerial ranking, giving them status equal to that of the Minister of Commerce. Large SOEs also have numerous affiliates whose roles range from carrying out social functions, such as providing jobs for employees with obsolete skills, to being publicly listed on Western stock exchanges such as the New York Stock Exchange. For example, although SASAC owns 64 per cent of CNOOC's equity, it is the 36 per cent publicly held affiliate that pursues transactions in North America. It might be that SASAC makes the affiliate's business decisions on political grounds, but this seems rather unlikely since, although the political behaviour of the parent enterprise's CEO is evaluated by the Central Organization Department, he also is rated on commercial criteria such as profitability.[13] Moreover, CEOs of affiliates are responsible to their shareholders and other stakeholders, such as their foreign employees, and they are subject to the regulatory regimes of host countries.

In summary, although opaque governance is a problem, there is plenty of evidence that most Chinese enterprises' commercial objectives are similar to those of other multinationals: to access new markets and to acquire brands, technology, and management skills. A recent survey shows that, although early Chinese investments in energy resources might have been intended to direct supplies to the home market, the majority of recent investments have aimed to expand global supplies in response to world market prices.[14] As Chinese enterprises gain more international experience and higher profiles, market pressures and the scrutiny of informed and vigilant national regulators likely will encourage their greater transparency and alignment with best international practices. Nonetheless, extra effort seems to be needed to ensure that Chinese investors meet the concerns of host countries. Enterprises in technologically sensitive businesses such as telecommunications face particularly intense scrutiny. In the United States, for example, the chairman of the intelligence committee of the

House of Representatives released a report in 2012 alleging bribery and corruption on the part of certain Chinese firms and requested a review by the Federal Bureau of Investigation.[15] Chinese
media and regulatory pressures on Apple's Chinese operations in
April 2013 suggest tit-for-tat behaviour that adds to unease.

Chinese outward investment, particularly in the United States,
will continue to grow, and the world will have to learn to live with
these it. Yet transparent frameworks for scrutinizing large deals on
grounds of national interest and national security are essential,
along with competent and well-informed regulatory oversight.
The basic issue is one of bridging differences between economic
systems. The end goal should be to improve competitiveness and
contribute to the development of both China and the countries
in which it invests.

INTERNATIONALIZING THE RENMINBI

The other major channel of China's integration into the world
economy is the use of its currency, the RMB. Until recently the
RMB was used exclusively for domestic transactions, but numerous
policy reforms are clearing the way for its increased use in trade
and currency swaps with central banks abroad. Indeed, China's
growing economic dominance in trade and investment implies,
eventually, a commensurate role for its currency. Yet the policy
reforms necessary for this realization are hotly debated in Beijing
because of their potentially negative impact on exporters whose
interests have been well served by a stable, undervalued exchange
rate and by the stable low interest rates that go with it. Now, the
greater market determination of interest and exchange rates and
the easing of restrictions on the use of the RMB outside China,
beginning with Hong Kong, Singapore, and Taiwan, potentially
open the Chinese economy to market volatility and shocks origi-
nating from outside.

Currencies become attractive for international use for several
reasons. One is the size of a country's share of world trade and
output. Large size gives the country market power in denominating trade transactions and enhances the breadth and size of its

financial markets. Another reason is the sophistication, size, and openness of a country's financial markets, which allow financial balances to be converted with ease into other currencies or financial products through a wide variety of instruments. A third reason is low inflation, which assures investors that the currency will not lose its value. A currency can also have a variety of international uses: in the invoicing and settlement of trade transactions, as a medium of exchange, as a unit of account in denominating cross-border assets and liabilities, as a vehicle currency in foreign-exchange markets, and as a store of value, for both investors and central banks that accumulate foreign-exchange reserves.

As of 2010, however, according to the latest available data for such a comparison, the RMB accounted for less than 1 per cent of all turnover in foreign-exchange markets. This was up from nothing a decade earlier, but still only a fraction of that accounted for by the pound Sterling, yen, euro, or US dollar. The domestic logic of internationalizing the RMB is to reduce borrowing costs and foreign-exchange risks for Chinese companies. For China's central bank, denominating trade finance in convertible RMB reduces the otherwise necessary inflow of US dollars and reduces market pressures for appreciation.

Encouraging China's large, earnings-rich enterprises to expand their activities abroad through outward investment also reduces demand pressures on the RMB. Reducing the demand for US dollars also reduces the amount China pays in seigniorage to the US Federal Reserve. China has the unique advantage of Hong Kong as an international financial centre where cross-border use of the RMB can be liberalized in controlled ways by permitting exporters and overseas institutions to open RMB-denominated accounts for trade settlement and permitting residents to use the RMB for outward foreign direct investment.

International use of the RMB in trade has grown quickly in recent years, advancing from thirty-fifth among world payment currencies in October 2010 to fourteenth in August 2012. Trade finance is the primary driver of this growth,[16] but it used more in invoicing for imports than for the settlement of exports.[17] One possible reason for this asymmetry is that foreign traders see opportunities for arbitrage and perhaps anticipate an appreciating RMB. Another reason could relate to China's reliance on oil imports, which are denominated in US dollars.

Balanced against the benefits of increasing RMB-denominated trade finance is that the currency's internationalization also opens the Chinese economy in important ways and increases its vulnerability to external shocks. A flexible exchange rate is required, which, in turn, requires market-determined interest rates. Such changes therefore must be made with care in a bank-dominated financial system like China's, where banks are mainly focused on the local market, lending is low risk, with riskless spread income coming from administered deposit and lending rates. How good are Chinese banks at anticipating and managing market risk, strategic risk, operational risks? How knowledgeable are they about offering domestic and foreign investors the choice of financial instruments that is available in more mature markets?

These observations and questions lead to another determinant of an international currency: a deep, sophisticated, and open financial system that attracts international investors seeking portfolio diversification. Although the RMB is growing in importance in trade, and although China has some of the world's largest banking institutions, as measured by market capitalization and capital, it still has a very long way to go in terms of the sophistication of the financial products available, the openness of its banking and capital markets, and the size and sophistication of its capital markets. None of the Chinese banks yet measures up to the major Western banks in international financial intermediation. So despite the contribution of Western financial institutions to the 2008 financial crisis, they are likely to continue to dominate international finance because of their huge global networks.

Chinese regulators are aware of these issues, and are gradually moving to free up many restrictions and weaknesses, while taking advantage of access to Hong Kong as an international financial centre. Integration into a regional bond market began in 2007 with the issue of "panda" bonds by the Asian Development Bank and the International Finance Corporation for use by foreign-funded enterprises in China; more recently the Ministry of Finance and the large banks have issued RMB bonds in Hong Kong, and international corporations have issued "dim sum" bonds. All of these moves are helping to create an offshore market with a benchmark rate for RMB debt instruments. Now, individuals, Hong Kong financial institutions, and mutual funds are permitted to have RMB deposits; as a consequence, the RMB is gaining a foothold in Hong Kong. The managed exchange-rate regime has also become more flexible in the past couple of years. The central bank is also pursuing currency swap programs with southeast Asian and other countries, which will facilitate the settlement of payments for exports in RMB.

But other conditions are needed to deepen the Hong Kong and offshore markets. In the early days of the eurodollar market, there was strong external demand for the US dollar because it was already in wide circulation, which made it an attractive market for foreign banks, and the US Federal Reserve was willing to provide unlimited dollar-clearing services. Today payments in US dollars can be settled in seconds. Market-clearing platforms are gradually being enhanced for the RMB, and some argue that the primary goal of such a clearing system should be the seamless routing of the RMB, both in China and globally. Most offshore RMB transactions are processed by the Bank of China in Hong Kong, a capability that is being expanded to Taipei, London, and Singapore.[18]

Yet, are international investors pushing to hold and invest large balances in RMB – that is, to use it as a store of value? Are Hong Kong banks finding the RMB business profitable? For that to be a reality, foreigners must be able to invest freely in RMB stocks, bonds, and bank deposits and to move their capital and earnings across borders. They must be convinced that market participants are well regulated and credible, and that market forces prevail. And, of course, for that to happen, capital account transactions need to be liberalized fully, and investors must be confident that Chinese financial markets are reasonably free of government interference.

The Chinese government is moving cautiously on exchange-rate flexibility and interest-rate liberalization, but significant institutional questions remain. If interest rates are to become market determined, what does this mean for a central bank that operates under political direction, or for state ownership and direction of commercial banks as instruments of industrial and development policy? Closely linked is the need to strengthen and modernize capital market institutions, particularly the creation of a sound, credible enterprise bond market and transparent, credible equity markets. It requires a deposit insurance system, exit channels for financial institutions that fail, and more sophisticated instruments to mitigate the risks of potentially large and volatile financial flows. All of these are needed if China's financial system is to produce globally competitive financial products and still thrive in an environment with full capital account convertibility.

The many restrictions that have been eased or removed in the past two years point in the right direction. The use of the RMB as an invoicing currency for trade transactions is now widespread, but there is still a long way to go before the RMB becomes a global medium of exchange and store of value, and a credible alternative to the US dollar. The Chinese view this as inevitable, and unlike the Japanese and the Germans, they are not reluctant to see their currency in international use. All China has to do is wait. But the wait could be long given the structure of China's trade – significant imports, including oil, continue to be denominated in US dollars – the need to strengthen and modernize the financial system, and the desirability of greater external and domestic demand. How long will it take to open the capital account fully, reform monetary policies, and develop world-class financial institutions?

The more likely path lies through RMB "regionalization" with China's neighbours, particularly ASEAN, with which it has a free trade agreement and whose members have incentives to denominate trade and financial transactions in RMB and to hold RMB in their reserves. This would still require financial market opening and deregulation in China, but less extensive than that required for the RMB to become a global currency.

In summary, China's integration into the world economy has been relatively smooth and well managed. Openness to world trade and investment has had positive effects on Chinese real incomes and on the choices available to the world's consumers. Similarly in foreign direct investment: China now has the resources to become one of the world's largest outward investors, and its investments, many of which include a premium for sellers and their shareholders, are saving jobs in countries hurt by the global recession and are helping to bring new resources to world markets, although Chinese SOEs still have much to learn about international business and host country market-based regulatory regimes.

But there are areas of concern. As a relative newcomer, with cherished goals of restoring its historical pre-eminence in Asia and commanding respect as a Great Power, China's increasing encounters with its neighbours and the United States are causing mounting unease. Already, the Pentagon has expressed its concerns about the malign intentions of the Chinese government and military to "plunder" US technology. Chinese officials have condemned such a suggestion, insisting that China is a victim, too, and offering to discuss issues of Internet security with the US government. Another source of unease is the lack of reciprocity in the treatment of foreign firms; their access to Chinese markets is generally more restricted than is Chinese access to their home markets. Yet another uncertainty is about the adjustments that might follow in international asset positions of SOE affiliates when parent firms' retained earnings shrink as they lose their subsidized inputs and as dividend payments rise. Will they be forced to sell foreign assets to raise cash?

Two particular concerns stand out. One is China's environmental impact now that the country is the world's largest emitter of greenhouse gases. There are strong domestic pressures to clean up, which have spurred innovation and opened the prospect of China's becoming a first mover in green industries. Success there, in turn, will spur international competition and innovation. The second concern is China's assertive behaviour in the Asian region and what this means for its strategic relations with the United States. I close this chapter with a discussion of these issues.

ENERGY AND THE ENVIRONMENT

China is the world's largest energy user and emitter of carbon dioxide – even in per capita terms its annual emissions are above the world average[19] – and 70 per cent of its energy needs are supplied by coal. Although it is the second-largest producer of wind power after the United States, solar and wind sources account for less than 1 per cent of its energy needs.

This fossil fuel-intensive footprint is largely determined by the economics of catch-up, whereby producers have relied on existing energy-intensive and polluting technologies in the dash for growth. Subsidized energy prices, moreover, have contributed to the overuse of such energy sources. Until 1998 there was no champion of the environment in the Chinese bureaucracy. The State Environmental Protection Administration was then set up, but as it was not a full-fledged ministry it lacked clout in dealing with powerful energy ministries. It was upgraded to the Ministry of Environmental Protection in 2008, and China's environmental policies have evolved from reacting to events such as floods and sandstorms and reliance on command-and-control techniques of regulation towards a coherent reform agenda based on the use of market forces to promote "green growth." Driving the shift have been such factors as the reform emphasis on innovation and productivity growth, a growing awareness that fast growth no longer requires high carbon intensity, and the potential benefits of becoming a leader in internationally tradable green technologies.

To realize these advantages, however, China will have to overcome the inertia of past policies. The incentives of local officials will have to change; until recently promotions were based on their contributions to growth, but in future they will have to depend more on their contributions to the *quality* of growth. Regulation, rather than pricing, has been the preferred environmental policy instrument, so that producers have found it advantageous to ignore regulations unless it was less costly to comply. Reports are rife of companies buying pollution-abatement equipment but failing to install it if the running costs are too high, or operating it only during visits by environmental inspectors. Data on pollution frequently are falsified, as a prominent example in Beijing has shown. Officials there manipulated data to downplay the serious health hazards of air pollution in the city, and it was only after the US embassy began announcing its own, much worse findings and under subsequent public pressure that the authorities adopted a higher standard. The US embassy nevertheless continues to publish its own readings.[20]

The Chinese government's concern for a cleaner environment, however, is gradually changing. With its greater political clout, the Ministry of Environmental Protection is improving its coordination of policies and changing incentive frameworks in other ministries. Penalties for pollution have increased, and there is more emphasis on the need to raise the prices of water, electricity, and coal to reduce their overuse. Consumers who purchase energy-efficient products are now eligible for subsidies. Environmental discharge permits are being issued, and carbon pricing and emissions trading mechanisms are the subject of increasing policy discussion.

This new concern for environmental quality has also been incorporated into the Twelfth Five-Year Plan, whose green reform strategy includes compulsory targets to reduce energy intensity by an estimated 16-to-18 per cent during the Plan period and carbon intensity by 40-to-45 per cent by 2020. Reliance on renewable energy sources is also to be increased to 15 per cent of total energy consumption by 2020.[21] Market-based measures through pricing reforms, new standards, and enforcement measures will also be introduced. The Plan further envisages the creation of "green cities," with Suzhou and Hangzhou selected for pilot projects.[22] A green growth "knowledge platform" has also been proposed that would monitor progress on such indicators as environmental and resource productivity, make estimates of the environmental assets base, measure the effects of environment quality (or the lack of it) on people's lives, and monitor the effects of policies to deliver green growth.[23]

CHINA'S BOUNDARY ISSUES IN ASIAN WATERS

Assertive boundary claims in the East and South China seas have called into question years of political stability and friendly diplomacy in Asia, the foundation stones of China's economic development and wealth generation. The dispute with Japan in the

East China Sea is perhaps the most serious threat to international peace because of Japan's naval capability to respond. The latest dispute began after three of five islets known to Japan as Senkaku and to China as Daioyu were purchased from their private owners in 2012 by a radical Tokyo municipal government. When the Japanese government nationalized them to exert greater control, China exploited the act at a time of political sensitivity around its own leadership transition. This unexpected string of events interrupted a tacit agreement by which Japan agreed not to carry out construction on the islets or allow anyone to land there in return for China's agreeing not to press its historical claim to them – many Chinese believe mention of the islands in ancient archives is sufficient evidence that they belong to China. The tacit agreement has held for more than forty years, although disputes occasionally have broken out over intrusions by fishing boats from the two countries. In a 2011 dispute, however, China upped the ante, retaliating against Japanese treatment of a Chinese fishing boat captain by restricting exports of rare earth minerals to Japan. Then, in 2012, protestors targeted Japanese products and production facilities in China, causing substantial physical and economic damage and lost sales. The two governments eventually calmed tensions, but in both countries, whose relationship is characterized by historical mistrust, new leaders are under pressure to prove their resolve to deter foreign threats. With sensitivities running high, the danger of accident and miscalculation is real.

China's claims in the South China Sea have both competitive and geopolitical implications. Competition is for oil and natural gas and access to the area's rich fishing grounds. China asserts its rights to as much as 90 per cent of the South China Sea within a boundary it claims has historical validity. Recently the public security ministry even inserted a map showing this boundary in the liner of new Chinese passports, inflaming passions in the region's smaller countries by ignoring not only their respective claims but also their two-hundred-mile Exclusive Economic Zones. Unlike Japan, moreover, they are not capable of fighting back. China is alleged to have cut an underwater cable of a Vietnamese vessel in waters claimed by Vietnam, and it has been in a standoff with the Philippines over Chinese fishing boats that entered a lagoon of the Scarborough Shoal, well within the Philippines' Exclusive Economic Zone.[24] When the Philippines government refused to withdraw from the Shoal, large shipments of tropical fruit to China were quarantined or subjected to go-slow inspections.

An enquiry into the causes of the conflict by an independent non-governmental organization, the International Crisis Group (ICG), emphasized the importance of conflicting mandates and the lack of coordination among numerous Chinese government agencies seeking to increase their power and budgets, including the navy's use of the maritime tensions to justify its modernization ambitions. The foreign ministry is the only one with a mandate to coordinate, but lacks the authority and resources to do so. The growing numbers of law-enforcement and paramilitary vessels in the area are there without a legal framework. The ICG notes that, although Beijing partially justifies its claims on the basis of the United Nations Convention on the Law of the Sea, it relies heavily on its own historical claims and boundary lines that it has not explained clearly.[25]

China prefers to manage such tensions in bilateral negotiations where, of course, it can rely on its size. But it has also engaged with the ASEAN and signed up to "Guidelines for the Implementation of the Declaration of Conduct in the South China Sea." This is an important step, but one ASEAN views as requiring follow-up with negotiations and specific measures. The geopolitical significance of these developments derives from the unease and mistrust unleashed by the foreign policy fiasco involving China's many agencies. In response, alarmed neighbours have turned to the United States to ask that it become more involved in the region as a counterbalance. Then-Secretary of State Hillary Clinton, hoping to help stabilize relations while avoiding direct US involvement, publicly encouraged claimants in the disputes to rely on legal evidence and channels. President Xi moved to soften the tone of relations with immediate neighbours when he received the 2013 ASEAN Chair and officials began to speak of "mutual benefit." But Xi insisted on settling disputes bilaterally. Not surprisingly, these events have had a serious effect on strategic relations, especially on China's relationship with the United States, the central topic of the next four chapters.

5 Twenty-First-Century Rivalry? Chinese and US Views of Each Other

[S]trategic distrust appears to be more the accepted wisdom in Beijing than in Washington.

– Kenneth Lieberthal and Wang Jisi[1]

In his book *Same Bed, Different Dreams* US political scientist David Lampton describes the management of the US-Chinese relationship in the period between 1989 and 2000 as a "double bet" in which China's leaders gambled that the United States would support their strategy of reform and opening to make China both wealthier and more influential in the global and regional economic and political environments fostered by Washington. In turn US leaders gambled that a wealthier China would become enmeshed with the rest of the world through growing economic ties and more liberal and supportive of the global system as a "responsible stakeholder," a term in common use today.[2]

Others do not share this view. Rather, they see the relationship as the latest in the history of rising and established powers, mainly European, that is plagued by competition, tension, and conflict. They expect that China inevitably will challenge US global hegemony, and that the United States will resist. Indeed, such dire prophecies can become self-fulfilling, but in a world of nuclear weaponry and deep economic integration they seem simplistic and as failing to recognize the braking effect that today's deep economic interdependence can have on armed conflict. Shooting at one's neighbour or major trading partner amounts to shooting oneself in the foot.

Complex economic and political relationships can be managed on many levels of state and non-state interaction – bilateral, regional, and multilateral. Most important in this bilateral relationship is that the two powers share the common imperative to address formidable domestic economic challenges. Failure to restructure their economies can only sow the seeds of future social and political tensions and social conflict at home. Both countries' publics are remarkably ignorant of each other despite their growing interaction and mutual obsession. Deepening mutual understanding and confidence are the basis of greater trust and cooperation, beginning with understanding how each views itself and the other.

How is the "double bet" unfolding?

HOW CHINESE VIEW THEMSELVES

Chinese views of themselves are complex. On the one hand are the exceptionalist historical narratives. As the Middle Kingdom, China's cultural and technological capabilities were without peer. Friendly commercial exchanges with its Asian neighbours were based on their acknowledging the emperor's superiority. Such memories colour China's geopolitical strategy in the region even today. In the early fifteenth century Admiral Zheng He commanded the largest naval fleet the world had ever seen, travelling the established trading routes of the time, and carrying out diplomatic explorations as well as commercial exchanges. At the same time, the humiliation narrative of siege and foreign exploitation runs through Chinese politics and drama to this day. Admiral Zheng's missions ended in 1433 – thirty-seven years before Portuguese explorers reached Africa's Gold Coast – when Chinese bureaucrats abruptly restricted commerce.[3] By the middle of that century, they were engaged in resisting Mongol border incursions by extending the Great Wall, a futile military gesture in the view of historian John Fairbanks, but illustrative of Chinese siege mentality.[4] In the nineteenth century Western powers and Japan exploited China's internal dissension and strife with incursions that caused a "century of humiliation and foreign exploitation."

This residual victim mentality was evident at the 2012 London Summer Olympics, when two Chinese athletes became the subject of international press commentary. In the first incident gymnast Chen Yibing put in what appeared to be a flawless performance yet was passed over for the gold medal by a Brazilian athlete whose performance many Chinese saw as flawed. In the second incident sixteen-year-old swimmer Ye Shiwen's unusually speedy performance and gold medal were attributed by some to drug use, of which Chinese swimmers often were guilty in the 1990s. These incidents led to an outburst of furious commentary in the Chinese press about "robbery" and racism such that the Party's Propaganda Department had to issue calming guidance. The *Beijing News* is reported to have urged its readers "to forsake the victim complex" and adopt a mentality more suited to a world power. *China Youth News* made similar observations.[5]

A strong sense of vulnerability underlies this humiliation narrative, which is also deeply entrenched in the thinking of China's defence and security establishments. One cause is the contested nature of China's borders, which it shares with such powers as Russia and India. It also shares a maritime border with Japan in the East China Sea, and claims Taiwan as a Chinese province. The region's geopolitical relationships are also complex, with South Korea, Japan, the Philippines, and Australia all having security alliances with the United States.[6]

Not surprisingly, topping China's list of international goals is the restoration of international respect and prominence. This aspiration is reflected in populist expressions of China's superiority, commonly heard in the wake of the global financial crisis as the realization dawned that China's economy eventually would become the world's largest. Such expressions can be understood in the context of the rapid transformation that has occurred in the lives of so many Chinese. One way of dealing with the resulting disorientation is to resort to familiar traditional conformist thinking. In such thinking there is little room for diverse views. The Chinese way must be the correct way; China's superior economic performance therefore should command the world's respect.[7]

Aspirations of respect, even of dominance, are evident in China's recent relationships with its Asian neighbours. For some years now, Chinese diplomats have articulated their country's "core interests," a concept that analysts trace and date to a July 2009 session of the US-China Strategic and Economic Dialogue, when State Councillor Dai Bingguo laid out these interests as preserving China's basic state system and national security, protecting national sovereignty and territorial integrity, and continued stable development.[8] The status of Taiwan is central to these interests, as are the sovereignty-related issues of Tibet and Xinjiang. At other times the concept has been applied to independence, human rights, and national unity, concepts that reinforce this core triad. Japanese reports assert that the issue of conflicting claims to the Senkaku/Diaoyu islets was also added in April 2013.[9]

Territorial claims in the South China Sea are not on the list. Yet, as we saw in Chapter 4, China's assertion of its claims has backfired, its bullying rhetoric and actions producing what Chinese most wish to avoid – namely, greater instability and volatility in regional relationships. Three decades of friendly foreign policy in Asia seemed to end when, at a 2010 meeting of the Association of Southeast Asian Nations (ASEAN) Regional Forum in Hanoi, Foreign Minister Yang Jiechi responded to complaints about China's claims by pointedly reminding participants that China is a big state, and that the others are smaller countries that should be grateful for the prosperity their proximity to China has brought them.[10] The investigation of incidents in the South China Sea by the independent International Crisis Group concluded that a wide range of Chinese interests beyond its navy have become involved in the area, each pursuing its own power objectives in an uncoordinated manner.[11] This apparent insensitivity to its neighbours and the expansion of its activities thus have become sources of deepening concern and mistrust. US re-engagement in the region further complicated matters, with high-level US officials energetically calling for "forward-deployed diplomacy" and "pivot." Both countries subsequently have adjusted course, with Dai Bingguo attempting to soothe passions in the region and US officials modifying their strategy to one of "rebalancing."[12]

HOW CHINESE VIEW AMERICANS

Chinese views of Americans also range across a wide spectrum. Significantly, while many have seen the United States as a point of reference, even a model, views have shifted to scepticism in the wake of the global financial crisis. Younger Chinese policy analysts are attracted to the "realist" international relations paradigm, developed and widely used in Western political science, that predicts that an established power will not accept a rising power, but instead will seek to weaken and influence its ruling regime. They regard the United States as a wounded superpower in decline, warlike, unpredictable, and determined, no matter how closely they might cooperate, to contain China's rise. To them arguments for deeper cooperation are self-defeating, the United States' political gridlock and diffuse power confusing: why is a president unable to implement his decisions on priority matters? They argue that China is being too passive in the face of what they see as the hostile trend of US rebalancing. Older Chinese, meanwhile, frame China's relationship with the United States in terms of Marxist class struggle; since the United States is bellicose, unpredictable, and determined to hem China in, China should stand up to it, even intervene abroad to protect Chinese interests.[13]

A continuing source of unease is the US "omnipresence" in China's perceived areas of vulnerability through its air and naval units, its formal and informal military alliances, and as the "primary framer and defender of existing international legal regimes." The extent of this presence persuades many Chinese policy makers that it amounts to restraint, even Cold War containment, despite demonstrated US actions to support Chinese prosperity.[14] Often lost in the sequence of recent events is a series of US actions that the Chinese government clearly sees as hostile. One is the White House decision to receive the Dalai Lama in 2010 and again in 2011. Another is the US announcement of a US$6 billion arms sale to Taiwan. As well, although little noticed in the United States, President Obama's 2011 speech to the Australian parliament was seen in China as unnecessarily critical and provocative, advocating regime change and criticizing China's achievements by asserting that "prosperity without freedom is just another form of poverty."[15]

Few Asian countries pine for a return to China's ancient tributary system; they, too, have memories of the colonial past and sensitivities about infringements, by Asians or others, on their hard-won sovereignty. Although they might wish for US support, they also do not want the United States to go so far as to force them into a position in which they must choose between China and the United States.[16]

Chinese liberals and internationalists hold more optimistic views. The "peaceful development" strategy adopted in 2003 assumes the United States will remain globally dominant for the foreseeable future, so a stable relationship is essential; it also recognizes the importance of Asia to China's development, so good relations with neighbours are essential, both to China and, given US stakes there as well, to increase China's leverage with the United States.[17] Some argue that, above all, there should be closer cooperation with the United States, but on the equal footing of two Great Powers that together shape global foreign policy.[18] Internationalists in think tanks and economic institutions argue for engagement with the US administration and for China to be more "creatively involved" in global institutions.[19]

Taken together, these diverse views suggest a possible shift in Chinese foreign policy thinking towards more assertiveness, shedding Deng Xiaoping's hide-and-bide, non-interventionist stance and moving to protect Chinese interests in the world, including those of the fifty-million-strong Chinese diaspora. A recent survey of intellectuals' views concludes with the observation that the big question for China's new leaders is, will they transcend pressures from nationalists and vested interests and conduct the mature foreign policy expected of a Great Power?[20]

HOW AMERICANS VIEW THEMSELVES AND CHINESE

Americans' views of China range across a wide spectrum. At one end are those who believe in US exceptionalism – and therefore refuse to acknowledge the narrative of Chinese exceptionalism. They believe in the moral superiority of US liberal, democratic values and individualism, and feel that the absence of such values in China makes Chinese leaders anxious and insecure about their legitimacy. Accordingly, they argue that an active campaign should exploit those insecurities and replace the authoritarian regime with a democracy.[21] Many Americans also see China as a threat. They believe China has a "grand strategy" to displace the United States and install itself as the hegemon of an exclusive Asian bloc.[22] For them, a fundamental divergence of interests is inescapable and détente impossible.

At the other end of the spectrum are Americans who interpret China's strategic goals in terms of its core interests; it follows that China would seek to reduce the dangers of geographic encirclement, re-establish a favoured position in Asia, resolve the Taiwan issue, and extend its economic and political presence in the developing world. To them the implication for US policy is to accept the reality of China's geopolitical prominence while maintaining the United States' Asian presence.[23]

Other thoughtful observers express concerns about the opacity of China's defence policies. They argue that building trust and mutual understanding requires transparency and reciprocal exchanges that give each side better understanding of the goals and strategies of the other, without necessarily leading to obstruction or containment. US defence budgets, for example, are posted to the Internet in official annual budgets. In contrast, about its own defence spending – now the world's second largest and growing at 12 per cent annually since 1989[24] – China provides little detail on allocations to research, new weapons systems, or personnel, although the 2013 report was more forthcoming about the size, deployment, and missions of its armed forces. These included missions relating to China's core interests as well as its contributions to peacekeeping, disaster relief, and international cooperation.[25] Chinese anti-satellite missiles, its first aircraft carrier, and the development of anti-access/area-denial capabilities, have caused alarm but, as Henry Kissinger has observed, "it would be unusual if the world's second-largest economy did not translate its economic power into increased military capacity."[26] Still, to allay suspicions, more transparency on China's part would add to the predictability that is valued in a potential partner, especially when it appears intent on enhancing its own capabilities while shrinking from contributing to global security.

THE DANGERS OF MUTUAL IGNORANCE AND MISCALCULATION

The range of views on both sides suggests substantial potential for misunderstandings and miscalculations that add to bilateral tensions. Foremost among these is the US strategic rebalancing towards Asia that has been under way since 2010, but here some Chinese confuse cause and effect. They tend to see the Trans-Pacific Partnership (TPP) trade initiative as part of that rebalancing when, in fact, the George W. Bush Administration had applied in 2008 to join an ambitious free trade agreement negotiated among four small countries in the Pacific and Latin America (New Zealand, Brunei, Chile, and Singapore). The initiative was designed to accept new members provided they were willing to commit to a comprehensive high-quality negotiation – a condition intended to raise the bar in Asian free trade agreements closer to the ideal of the World Trade Organization. As other countries have joined, however, the Chinese have developed a narrative whereby the TPP is designed to exclude China, even though China has not asked to join. As well, the increased US naval presence and military exercises in the area that so alarm some Chinese are only a modestly larger deployment above US practice over the past six decades. Some Chinese also believe that the United States, by joining the East Asia Summit backstopped by ASEAN, is "intervening in Asia-Pacific affairs."[27]

Americans are subject to misapprehensions of their own. US presidential candidate Mitt Romney, for example, appeared to assume a unipolar world in the 2012 campaign when he threatened that, "unless China changes its ways, on day one of my presidency I will designate it a currency manipulator and take the appropriate action." This promise, which Romney's election loss made moot, could have had serious consequences if carried out. The legislative basis for carrying out such a charge exists: it would trigger immediate negotiations between treasury officials in the two countries. If these had led to nothing but a war of words, Congress then could gotten into the fray and adopted legislation authorizing countervailing tariffs on trade with "currency manipulators," something it has repeatedly threatened to do in any case. In tracing through the likely consequences of Chinese-US tit-for-tat responses in trade and finance, China expert Stephen Roach suggests that, eventually, growth rates would plunge in both countries and unemployment would rise; the global economy would slip back into recession and rumours would circulate of a replay of the Smoot Hawley tariff that triggered the Great Depression.[28] Such is the possible price of a public commitment made for short-term political advantage that could haunt a newly elected leader.

Romney's threat illustrates a lack of sensitivity in the US policy community to China's humiliation narrative and its expectation to be dealt with respectfully in accordance with its stable and peaceful re-emergence as a global power. US rhetorical admonitions for China to become a responsible stakeholder ignore these expectations. At the same time, Chinese should realize that it is time to "move on" and to assume the mantle of a mature global power, as the *Beijing News* and *China Youth Daily* counselled during the 2012 London Summer Olympics. In short, avoiding misinterpretations requires better communication within a strategic framework that accepts and defines the presence of both countries in the region and promotes better coordination.[29]

This does not mean that firm lines should not be drawn – on China's alleged currency manipulation, for example. China has kept its currency undervalued by intervening in the foreign-exchange market – but so have others in managing their currencies including Denmark, Hong Kong, Malaysia, Singapore, Switzerland, Taiwan and some oil exporters. Adjustment measures range from cooperation by countries with surpluses to unilateral actions by countries with deficits, such as countervailing currency market intervention, taxes on foreign-exchange buildup, and countervailing duties or import surcharges.[30] Romney's confrontational campaign rhetoric, in contrast, amounts to megaphone diplomacy. Relying on multilateral forums and bilateral consultations and negotiations if necessary is a superior, but more time- and resources-intensive process.

Lines can also be drawn with smarter strategic policy. China's security establishment, for example, could overplay its hand in the boundary disputes or downplay the role of the United States as the region's "resident power." Assertive Chinese behaviour could provoke a US reaction that, in one scenario, would not be a conventional display of "hard power" but "mischief" that stirs up unwanted economic instability – for example, by creating instability in the sea lanes through which China's vital energy supplies are transported, or inducing investor panic at the prospect of rising regional tensions.[31]

IMPLICATIONS

When strategic mistrust colours the relationship, the dangers of miscalculations increase. Prophecies can become self-fulfilling if their assumptions and outcomes are uncritically accepted. But nothing is inevitable. A critical look behind the generalities encoded in headlines provides a much more nuanced picture of two economic powers with markedly different cultural and historical roots and a remarkable variety of views of each other – and of what each believes the other thinks of it – but with common economic constraints and priorities. Each is constrained by its economic interdependence with the other. The United States is dependent on Chinese savings to finance its public deficits as long as it fails to bring spending in line with revenues; China is dependent on the jobs created by goods exports to high-income US consumers, since its own consumers, with per capita incomes a tenth of those of Americans, cannot replace any time soon.

The end game should be a "normal" major power relationship in which economics trumps military thinking. Getting along with each other well enough so that each can focus on its domestic imperatives should be the goal. Both should move to build mutual confidence through deeper understanding of the other's core interests and accommodating each other's deepest fears. President Xi Jinping, in a public address in Washington on 15 February 2012, called for building a "cooperative partnership" based on mutual understanding and respect for each other's core interests and concerns, and on economic and international cooperation. The Obama Administration believes a constructive bilateral relationship is possible and that conflict can be avoided, as then-Secretary of State Hillary Clinton avowed in her expressions of confidence in a "strong prosperous and peaceful China." Both sides must work towards greater transparency and the building of deeper understanding and mutual confidence.

Given the importance of these precedents, the decision of Clinton's successor, John Kerry, to make his first foreign trip to Europe and the Middle East sent a confused signal. Former US diplomats frame the challenge of creating a normal relationship with China in terms of reconciling Chinese fears of encirclement or containment with US fears of Chinese insistence on hegemony. For both to achieve their objectives without resorting to military conflict, Americans need to accept the new realities of China's major influence in Asia even as the United States modifies its strategy, now two generations old, of guarding the region against nuclear war to one of deterring potential aggressors. Both sides, in short, need to understand the fears of the other and to "define the sphere in which their peaceful competition is circumscribed."[32] As a former US ambassador to China asked in a recent roundtable, "Is there an array of military deployments and normal operations that will permit China to better defend its core interests while allowing the United States to continue to fully meet US defense commitments in the region?"[33] He and others with China experience argue that the almost exclusive emphasis on security has been a mistake. Economic rebalancing, where both sides win, can help offset fears through free trade initiatives that include China, unlike the TPP, which the Chinese criticize as pursuing high standards that effectively exclude China at this stage of its economic development. They also advocate turning down the loud military "soundtrack" and turning up the economic "soundtrack."

Much has been made in both countries of whether China now can move beyond Deng Xiaoping's assessment of superior US power and international status. Triumphalist Chinese commentators have celebrated the relative decline of the United States since the global financial crisis, China's successful navigation of that crisis, its rise to prominence as the successful host of the Olympics in 2008 and Shanghai Expo in 2010, and its recent advances in military and space technology. Yet public discussion in China reveals vagueness in the discourse about the country's possible global role and about writing new rules. There is little evidence of China's repudiating or replacing the existing global system, beyond periodic summits of the so-called BRICs (Brazil, Russia, India, and China) and the issuing of communiqués of their intention to cooperate on projects such as a new development bank. Instead, China has manipulated the existing rules to its own benefit.

The "double bet" has paid off so far, and although many Chinese remain suspicious and lacking in confidence, others think the time has come for China to stand up to the United States. Such pressures, however, distract China's leaders from acting in its best long-term interests. Both China and the United States can do better. They should invest in greater transparency about where they can cooperate and where they will compete. They should dial down the rhetoric, the United States on rebalancing and China on containment – although this does not mean the United States should not continue to ensure the security of friendly nations and allies. They should support the development of rules-based regimes and codes of conduct, particularly in the South China Sea. And for their part China's leaders should encourage popular thinking about China as a global power and look beyond the country's core interests.

Many international outlets exist where Chinese leadership can be displayed, including in coalitions of countries such as ASEAN and the BRICs. In following chapters I focus on the two channels where China has expressed the most interest: global institutions and its relationship with the United States. In the next chapter I examine China's record in multilateral economic institutions and the importance of the United States' making room for the rising power – and its setting a better example of respecting the rules it had a major role in crafting. As the door of opportunity opens to update these forums for the twenty-first century, China needs to cross the threshold.

6 China and Global Governance

With internal affairs high on the agenda, it is of great necessity for China to strike a balance between its national interests and international responsibilities, between self-development and a win-win development strategy with other countries. This will push relations between China and the world towards peace and cooperation. This will safeguard the national interests of China, and also determine whether China can offer solutions to global problems.

– Jin Canrong[1]

In the depths of the 2008 global financial crisis, a meeting of the leaders of just the Group-of-Seven (G7) countries would have been irrelevant. Instead the broader G20 came into play. The crisis highlighted the need to reshape the post-war governance institutions created by Western governments to represent the changing distribution of global economic power and rising economic interdependence.

China, however, has yet to play a significant role in this historic architectural transition. Despite its growing integration with the world economy, its leaders were surprised by the accelerating expectations of China in the wake of the financial crisis. They have articulated interest in and support for existing institutions, but have made few proposals for change. Until those changes occur, international cooperation will continue to be shaped by relative economic size, political tensions, and crises. Any transition to new institutions is likely to be gradual, but Asia's growing weight will

Figure 6.1. Changing Shares of Global Output, 2005–30

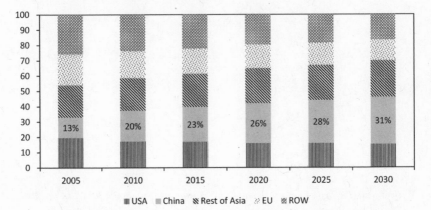

Notes: ROW is the rest of the world; rest of Asia includes Hong Kong, India, Indonesia, Japan, Malaysia, Pakistan, the Philippines, Singapore, South Korea, Taiwan, Thailand, and Vietnam; the GDP measure is constant 2005 US dollars, measured by purchasing power parity.
Source: Lee Jong-wha and Hong Kiseok, "Economic Growth in Asia: Determinants and Prospects," Economics Working Paper 220 (Tokyo: Asian Development Bank, September 2010), 27, available online at http://www.adb.org/publications/economic-growth-asia-determinants-and-prospects.

mean that, although the United States and the European Union will remain important centres of power, governance will be conditioned by Asian preferences for consensus decision making and for relationships over rules and legal frameworks.[2] In 2010 the shares of global output generated by the United States, China, the rest of Asia, and the European Union were roughly equal; over the next twenty years, however, the shares of China and the rest of Asia taken together are projected to increase to 60 per cent of the total (see Figure 6.1). This coming change in economic power has added weight to calls for revising the governance of the International Monetary Fund (IMF), the World Bank, and other global institutions to provide a stronger role for emerging economies.

China, however, is ambivalent about the governance implications of this shift. History is a powerful factor in its scepticism and distrust of global systems. Until well after the Second World War China's foreign contacts were based on sharply unequal power relations, and unresolved regional tensions remain close to the surface. Notably missing from Asia's complex network of bilateral free trade agreements is a link among China, Japan, and South Korea. Negotiations periodically are announced, but then fall prey to political events such as confrontations in the East China Sea. These intra-regional tensions help to explain why Asian countries depend on partnerships with extra-regional powers, including the United States, to insure against regional conflicts.

More broadly in Asia, the nascent mechanisms of cooperation reflect this complicated history. Commitment to the existing global economic governance framework is widespread, not least in China, which used its negotiations to accede to the World Trade Organization (WTO) to undertake sweeping domestic reforms.[3] The region's successful focus on economic development relies critically on peace and political stability – wealth, not bullets, has been the route to power and influence. But as China's economic power has grown, and with it investments in political and military influence, it has made mistakes, as in the South China Sea, while assuring neighbours that its markets and policies will continue to serve as a powerful regional locomotive. The absence of formal agreements among the region's leading economies leaves a power vacuum, however, with no country able to provide broad leadership. Sometimes China and Japan have even proposed competing regional integration initiatives forcing smaller countries into delicate balancing acts.

EVALUATING CHINA'S ROLE

China takes enormous pride in its independence and accomplishments even as it recognizes the benefits of global stability and interdependence. Its lack of participation reflects its relative inexperience with global institutions, its focus on domestic concerns, and an aversion to complex legal systems and international rules. China's position was articulated in 2006 by President Hu Jintao, when he called for peaceful development in a harmonious world (*hexie shijie*), which includes principles of independence, self-reliance, and peaceful coexistence, with differences resolved on the basis of mutual respect and cooperation. These principles do not envision conflict with the West, but they nevertheless challenge

Western views by omitting priorities such as human rights, democracy, transparency, and the rule of law.

Such Chinese critiques of international institutions lead to calls for, among other things, the United States to become a "normal" country and abide by international law; for Western countries to open their markets more to developing countries; and for greater reliance on the United Nations system in multilateral diplomacy and world peace. These critiques, however, overlap with Western views that the international order should be built on international regimes and on democratic decision making within international institutions, and should emphasize fairness, mutual respect, and development.[4]

Despite these overlapping prescriptions for the world order, much uncertainty remains about how such principles will translate into action as China's power grows: will it be able to provide leadership for global and regional institutions and still serve its domestic interests? In the United States and elsewhere, there is concern that China has done only the minimum requested, kept a low profile, and not played much of a role in discouraging countries from violating international norms of conduct. China's rising power and slow ascent to leadership are playing out in the context of an increasingly complex international agenda. There is growing demand for international public "goods" such as intergovernmental agreements and institutions to prevent or mitigate risks to peace, health, and the environmental commons, but little increase in the supply on the part of the current international system.

Traditionally, international public goods have been provided by strong and arguably relatively wealthy hegemonic leaders that have imposed rules and institutions through a combination of pressures and incentives. Britain in the nineteenth century and the United States in much of the twentieth played this role. Their economic size made it worth their while to offer significant benefits to other countries, such as access to markets, to encourage their participation in an open world order. In today's multipolar world, however, the provision of international public goods encounters the "free-rider" problem, whereby smaller economies prefer to benefit from access to others' markets without providing access to their own. As the relative power of the United States has declined, the prominence of free ridership has grown and the supply of international public goods has declined, notwithstanding the increased need for cooperation.

Chinese preferences and the logic of cooperation offer useful lenses through which to explore recent trends in China's role in global economic governance. A survey of the principal elements of the international governance architecture shows China's participation in most functional areas (see Table 6.1).

High-Level Cooperation

The most important public good required of the global system is high-level cooperation on problems that cut across major economies and fields of policy. When the financial crisis hit, the world had no such institution. Leaders had to meet urgently and develop new mechanisms to involve the expanding number of economies essential to the task. The G20 emerged in the heat of crisis with the world's largest economies and regional leaders as its members. Leaders focused initially on generating consistent national responses to the crisis and monitoring the actions of international organizations. They directed the IMF to provide appropriate emergency liquidity, strengthen its own monitoring functions, and reform its governance to reflect the changing shape of the global economy. They requested the WTO to monitor protectionist measures and to conclude the Doha Round of multilateral trade negotiations, and instructed the World Bank to mitigate the effects of the crisis on the poor in developing countries. The G20 leaders also transformed the Financial Stability Forum, which had been created in 1999, into a Financial Stability Board charged with developing new international rules for financial oversight. In time, progress was made on all of these tasks.

China is, of course, a central member of the G20. From early on, its exchange-rate and foreign-exchange reserve policies were the subject of criticism, which it deflected and to which it responded. Expressing support for the G20 forum in 2010, President Hu outlined priorities for shifting cooperation towards "long-term governance and from passive response to proactive planning." He

Table 6.1. China in Global Governance

Function and Institutions	Chinese Objectives
High-level cooperation (G20)	• Support global institutions • Move to a more representative system • Resist formal economic targets
Trade liberalization and dispute settlement (WTO, ASEAN+, regional agreements)	• Support global trade • Avoid legally binding disciplines • Wary of strong intellectual property rights • Assertive industrial policies • Interest in regional free trade agreements
Monetary and macroeconomic cooperation (IMF, Chiang Mai Initiative, ASEAN+3 Macroeconomic Research Office)	• Support global monetary oversight • Support governance reform • Gradual increase in RMB flexibility • IMF as provider of global reserve currency
Financial market oversight (Financial Stability Board)	• Relaxed view of international rules due to strong current position of banks
Development finance (World Bank, Asian Development Bank)	• Support development finance • Pursue Chinese aid program • Emphasize infrastructure, resource development • Emphasize political relationships
Climate change mitigation (UN Framework on Climate Change)	• Green growth a priority at home • Critical of developed countries' failures to fund development, mitigation • Pledges/plans to reduce carbon emissions based on development capacity

Source: Based on Petri and Dobson, "Asia in Global Economic Governance."

urged establishing "a new international financial order that is fair, equitable, inclusive and well-managed," and policies that "reject all forms of protectionism and unequivocally advocate and support free trade."[5] But aside from listing these objectives and pressing for the inclusion of its currency, the renminbi, in the IMF's Special Drawing Rights (SDRs, the Fund's accounting units), China has offered few concrete proposals. It has played no role in Asian calls for a regional strategy, although it has experimented with other alliances – for example, by joining dialogues of the BRICs (Brazil, Russia, India, and China).

Despite, or perhaps because of, its unique role in global governance, the G20 has been more successful in responding to crises than in delivering sustained cooperation. Its contribution has evolved for the time being into facilitating discussion, while standing by for emergencies – an operational model that mirrors Asian more than Western approaches to governance, and might be a harbinger of change in the global system.

Trade and Investment

China is not a leader in the WTO. One reason is that it considers it has "already given." Its fifteen-year accession negotiations were used as an instrument of domestic policy reform, transforming the institutions and managers of the planned economy into more market-oriented ones. Some terms were harsh – China accepted designation as a non-market economy in antidumping and safeguard cases and agreed to annual compliance reviews – but the concessions paid off. China is now a leading exporter and emerging market destination for foreign direct investment. A second reason is that its major markets for goods in developed economies are already reasonably open, while the liberalization of trade in services is not yet of comparable interest to China. Moreover, China sees the "new issues" – labour and environmental protection – as designed to undermine its own areas of comparative advantage.

Most global trade is conducted under WTO rules and institutions – with the addition of Russia in 2011, every large trading economy is now a member – and its dispute resolution mechanism is widely used and usually obeyed. Given the monitoring and safety valves it provides, protectionist responses to the global financial crisis appear to have been surprisingly muted. The WTO Government Procurement Agreement sets significant limits on government intervention through procurement, and is a nuanced indicator of the role of Asian economies in the WTO system. China has committed to join the agreement, but it took nine years, until 2010, to offer a negotiating proposal that remains under discussion.[6]

China and other Asian economies have also pursued regional trade initiatives, which are easier to manage because they focus mainly on tariff reductions on goods, allow exceptions, and treat lightly issues of more interest to advanced economies, such as services, intellectual property rights, investment, and labour. The free trade agreement between China and the Association of Southeast Asian Nations (ASEAN) has been a catalyst for other large Asian economies, with South Korea, Japan, and India following suit. Competing proposals have sought to expand these agreements beyond the ASEAN+3 (ASEAN, China, Japan, and South Korea) preferred by China to an ASEAN+6 (adding Australia, India, and New Zealand) proposed by Japan. In 2011, a truce negotiated by China and Japan permitted both initiatives to move forward in parallel. ASEAN is also developing its own blueprint for regional comprehensive economic partnerships, which is intended to harmonize all the ASEAN+ agreements and permit other countries to join. In practice, the success of these efforts will depend on consensus among China, Japan, and South Korea, the region's three largest economies.

Despite extensive efforts, little progress has been made towards a comprehensive regional agreement, which would produce results far superior to a series of smaller agreements.[7] Since benefits increase with the size of the area, ASEAN+6 would generate somewhat greater gains than ASEAN+3, and an agreement that included all twenty-one economies of the Asia-Pacific Economic Cooperation (APEC) forum – which includes the United States, Canada, and all other countries on the eastern edge of the Pacific – would be better still,[8] as the United States is a critical market for Asian manufactures and a potential stabilizing force in the face of China's rising power. The members of APEC agreed in 2008 to pursue a Free Trade Area of the Asia Pacific (FTAAP), a long-term goal to be reached by several alternative pathways.

The United States has also entered the negotiating arena by promoting the Trans-Pacific Partnership (TPP), which builds on a comprehensive, high-quality free trade agreement and intends to create a "twenty-first-century" standard for trade. Its ultimate bene-fits inevitably depend, however, on whether large Asian economies join, as Japan has decided to do; China has not indicated such a desire. In the meantime both the FTAAP and TPP tracks are gen-erating forward momentum on trade liberalization, yielding real benefits at low cost to non-members.[9] The tracks are a "contest of templates" designed to shape eventual patterns of integration.

Investor protection is a prominent feature of current trade ne-gotiations, since investment provides the linkages among regional production networks that are a key feature of the Asian economic architecture. Conflicting objectives – such as attracting foreign in-vestors while protecting the right to invest in sensitive resource and technology sectors abroad – make it difficult, however, to design a consistent investment regime. Some of the challenges Chinese investors face in foreign markets are illustrated by high-profile failures. Attempts at key resource acquisitions (China Na-tional Offshore Oil Corporation's of Unocal in the United States; Chinalco's of Rio Tinto's assets in Australia) failed for apparently political reasons. Chinese technology companies also face suspi-cion in India and the United States on national security grounds. US politicians have accused electronics giant Huawei of having military ties, and call for its access to the supply chains of the mili-tary and law enforcement sectors to be blocked. After several failed attempts to acquire US technology assets, Huawei announced in early 2013 its intention to seek new markets elsewhere.

China's own foreign investment regime has also raised con-cerns, as we saw in Chapter 4. Although open to many types of for-eign investment, China has often required technology transfers as a condition of market access. The conviction and imprisonment of foreign executives – including an Australian and an American, on charges of bribery in the first case and violating laws on state secrets in both cases – has raised serious concerns about interrela-tionships among business, politics, and the Chinese legal system, although such cases might have been retaliation for discrimina-tion against Chinese companies abroad. The complexity and im-portance of such investment linkages represents a clear argument for strengthening rules-based approaches.

These trends therefore raise conflicting questions. Will China continue to cede the leadership of the world trading system to the United States and Europe, as it did through much of the post-war period? Will it agree to deepen regional cooperation by participating in both the FTAAP and TPP tracks? A more prominent role for China is inevitable, but it likely will emerge gradually. Its scale and connections with the world economy suggest that purely regional, even broader Asia-Pacific, initiatives will not accommodate its interests. Eventually China, as dominant Western economies before it have done, is likely to emerge as a champion of a stable and open global system. The precise implications of this emergence are unclear, but the resulting order will need to bridge contemporary Western legal approaches with the flexible, relationship-based models of Asian integration.

Macroeconomic Cooperation

China is least ambivalent and most clearly internationalist in its participation in the international monetary system. So far it has worked within the system to advance its interests in a voice consistent with its economic size. It has long been a member of the IMF, whose mandate has changed over the years from being at the centre of a system of fixed exchange rates to promoting the international monetary cooperation necessary to maintain orderly exchange-rate arrangements and to expand world trade. The IMF conducts regular surveillance of members' macroeconomic policies, offers technical support, and provides short-term liquidity to members with balance-of-payments difficulties. Yet, when private capital flows overtook official flows by the mid-1990s, the IMF's resources shrank in relative terms and the nature of its borrowers changed – increasingly they were smaller developing countries with little say in how the Fund is run – while the advanced countries continued to dominate its decision making and determination of conditions on borrowers.[10]

These issues came to a head during the 1997 Asian financial crisis when, rightly or wrongly, the IMF was perceived to have deepened the crisis by treating Asian borrowers with liquidity problems as if they were insolvent with structural problems.[11] Resentful borrowers repaid their loans early and began self-insuring by accumulating foreign reserves larger than those needed to cover imports and short-term liabilities. By the time of the 2008 global financial crisis, the IMF's reduced resources and credibility problems were such that it was not a significant player. Its resources, at around US$250 billion, paled in comparison with those of Asia's central banks, whose foreign-exchange reserves totalled nearly US$5 trillion in 2010, and sovereign wealth funds, which were managing more than US$2 trillion in 2006.[12] Central banks, led by the US Federal Reserve, were also active in bilateral swap arrangements to address short-term liquidity problems. G20 leaders resuscitated the Fund by restoring its resources to US$1 trillion and encouraging it to set up new facilities to help countries solve their credit problems.[13] The IMF streamlined its lending framework and conditionality, providing adjustment support through short-term lending facilities through which countries qualifying on an *ex ante* basis can access loans immediately, and other credit lines on precautionary bases without conditions.[14]

Governance reforms agreed to at the G20 summit in Seoul in November 2010 will make China the third-largest shareholder in the IMF.[15] How will China use this increased clout? So far it has both dragged its feet and proposed reform. The slow adjustment of its nominal exchange rate has drawn strong US criticism, with some arguing that "rejection of a flexible exchange rate" is a direct challenge to the international monetary order.[16] China was also one of the last members, along with the United States, to agree to an evaluation by the IMF's Financial Sector Assessment Program, which focuses on national financial systems and their prudential supervision. At the same time China has actively pursued governance reforms to raise its voting strength and adopt SDRs as a super-sovereign reserve currency to provide an alternative way to reallocate its foreign-exchange reserves. Central bank governor Zhou Xiaochuan has argued that current arrangements, which rely on a single national currency, the US dollar, are flawed because of the potential for conflict between domestic goals and international responsibilities.[17] As the dollar-based system has become more volatile, developing and emerging market economies have diverted foreign-exchange reserves from more productive uses to self-insure. Using SDRs in this way would allow large holders of US government securities to diversify their holdings in the IMF, thereby avoiding exchange-market volatility.[18] The proposal has gained little traction, however, because of the entrenched position and convenience of the US dollar for use by both market participants and governments.

Regionally, China has been active in multilateralizing the Chiang Mai Initiative (CMIM), a regional emergency financing mechanism set up in 2000 to facilitate bilateral currency swap agreements among the members of ASEAN+3. By 2012 the CMIM had funding commitments totalling US$240 billion to provide short-term liquidity and balance-of-payments support in the region. But the difficult work of establishing procedures to activate the CMIM and provide associated surveillance has just begun; for now, substantial draws on CMIM funds will require an IMF program as well. An Asian Macroeconomic Research Office has been established in Singapore to support the CMIM. Ideally, it will develop procedures consistent with IMF methodology so that support might combine IMF and CMIM funds. Early indicators of the CMIM's effectiveness will be members' willingness to submit to multilateral peer review and surveillance of national policies and to reduce self-insurance.

Within China it is increasingly recognized that liberalizing such key prices as the exchange rate and interest rates are essential steps in its future strategy for sustained growth, as we saw in Chapter 3. International rebalancing is also necessary to ensure the safety of China's accumulated reserves, which will lose value as the US dollar depreciates or if US inflation picks up and US bond prices decline. In real terms, the RMB exchange rate has strengthened against the US dollar by almost 50 per cent since 2005 as Chinese prices have risen much faster than those in the United States. Change in the nominal rate, however, will be gradual and controlled, according to China's needs. Gradual RMB internationalization is also under way, as we saw in Chapter 4.

In summary, China is not only engaged in IMF governance; it has also proposed reforms. It has said "no" to outside pressures for exchange-rate appreciation, but it has participated in the G20's enhanced surveillance process, which relies on analysis by the IMF. There are two tests of China's recognition of the external effects of its domestic policy choices. One is its willingness to be transparent with respect to surveillance within the CMIM, where it is a major shareholder. The other test is political: whether re-balancing under the Twelfth Five-Year Plan includes a market-determined exchange rate despite political opposition, in order to develop a deep and liquid market-based financial system that uses capital more efficiently. China must pass both tests if it is to have an international impact commensurate with its modern and complex economy.

Financial-Market Oversight

The 2008 global financial crisis highlighted the paradox between the national scope of financial supervision and the global reach of capital markets and institutions. Although strong and modern national financial systems are essential to stable markets, national regulators acting on their own cannot prevent cross-border financial crises; they must coordinate and communicate among themselves. The Financial Stability Board, based at the Bank for International Settlements in Basel, Switzerland, and closely related to the Basel Committee on Banking Supervision, is meant to facilitate such cooperation, and is charged with working closely with the IMF to implement its recommendations and guidelines through the Fund's surveillance and its Financial Sector Assessment Program.

The 2010 Basel III Accords provide a new framework for bank regulation in the wake of the global financial crisis. Although China was involved in the discussions leading up to the accords, it did not play a central role in their design. For the most part its banks have not been unduly strained by the new regulations; in many cases asset structures were more conservative than those of Western banks and their equity positions stronger, so the implications of meeting the new standards are manageable. On the whole the accords have not increased calls for regional regulations, despite suggestions from the Asian Development Bank for a regional regulatory forum similar to the Financial Stability Board.

Development Finance

Since 1980 China has had a harmonious relationship with the World Bank and continues to borrow for projects ranging from energy efficiency and the environment to urban and rural development. In 2007 China became a net contributor to the World Bank's International Development Assistance mechanism and in 2010 its third-largest shareholder. A Chinese national served as the World Bank's chief economist between 2008 and 2012.

Development banks tend to have established dominant country personalities – for example, the Asian Development Bank, which is active in promoting regional integration among developing economies in southeast Asia by providing substantial support for new transportation corridors and other infrastructure initiatives, is led by the Japanese. Accordingly, with its massive foreign-exchange reserves, China could lead to some new directions in development lending, possibly through its own development bank. Already, an ASEAN-China Investment Cooperation Fund, announced in 2009, will focus on infrastructure development opportunities in the ASEAN region.[19]

China offers loans to member states of the Shanghai Cooperation Organization, a grouping of six economies in central Asia, and a variety of infrastructure investment support for African countries. China's sovereign wealth fund, the China Investment Corporation, is investing in infrastructure projects around the world, including in advanced countries such as the United Kingdom and the United States. These efforts represent an interesting new mix between initiatives designed to secure relatively safe and high returns, and China's relations with the host governments. They signal a shift from traditional lending functions towards direct investments in narrower asset portfolios that support its political and commercial interests.

The Environment

Owing to its rapid industrialization and large population, China faces serious environmental problems ranging from water availability and quality to air pollution and carbon dioxide emissions. It is now the world's largest producer of greenhouse gases, although not in per capita terms, and it is a reluctant participant, along with India, in negotiations to mitigate climate change. It remains committed to rapid economic growth, and relies heavily on fossil fuels and coal as industrial energy sources. It sees pressures to generate binding commitments on emissions, especially given vague commitments by much wealthier nations, as efforts to constrain its economic catch-up with the West. Indeed, the central issue is how to allocate responsibility for mitigation among countries. There is much rhetoric and little agreement on how emissions targets should be determined, and many questions. For example, should responsibility be allocated on the basis of emissions per capita, emissions per unit of gross domestic product (GDP), or absolute emissions? China prefers an emissions-per-GDP standard, because fast development reduces energy intensity by this measure, even as it increases other ratios. It also argues for taking past emissions into account, and for special treatment for developing countries through, for example, funds that support adaptation in poor countries.

Given such divisions, progress on negotiations on global climate change mitigation is bound to be limited. The Copenhagen Conference in December 2009 appeared to be headed for massive failure, but at the last minute Brazil, China, India, South Africa, and the United States agreed to a non-binding commitment to keep temperature increases under 2°C. Seen as a face-saving gesture, this agreement kept the negotiating process alive. At the Durban Conference in November 2011 China and the United States committed to negotiate to replace the Kyoto Protocol with a new treaty by 2015 and implemented by 2020. There was also some commitment to the principle of accepting binding mitigation targets. So far, however, pledges have been insufficient to meet global targets on emissions reduction – indeed, Chinese negotiators have indicated that they are not prepared to make larger concessions than they have already offered. As well, little progress has been made on funding the Green Climate Fund or on reducing deforestation emission and forest degradation.

The Chinese public, on the other hand, recognizes the harmful health effects of pollution and CO_2 emissions, and it is partly in response to these concerns that the Twelfth Five-Year Plan has obligatory targets to increase renewable energy supplies and reduce carbon intensity by 2020. China is making large investments to develop globally competitive wind and solar power industries that could lead to major innovations and new industries. These are also attracting US complaints of unfair trade, however; currently several US antidumping investigations are under way of Chinese exports of alternative energy products.

In short, China's stance on the environment is consistent with its ambivalence towards global economic governance: participate in global processes and apply the brakes to initiatives that might constrain its own options. At the same time, innovations are helping to make alternative energy an important growth industry, while concerns about energy security also argue for greater conservation efforts. All these factors could encourage more proactive Chinese policies, based as usual on pragmatic self-interest.

In conclusion, China's role in most institutions of global economic governance remains modest and its intentions unclear. As yet there is little evidence that it intends to reshape or undermine these institutions, although it clearly supports critiques of Western dominance and double standards and calls for these to change. China nevertheless shares many Western views on how the world economy works, as well as broad Western goals for macroeconomic and trade policy. It remains reluctant, however, to assume the costly responsibilities of global leadership or to invest more in international institutions than is justified by its domestic interests.

At the same time China's behaviour in Asian regional forums has consequences. Its assertive stance on boundary issues, for example, has backfired, undermining its regional leadership role. Indeed, China has little historical experience of cooperating with peers, and prefers bilateral over multilateral bargaining, where its clout is reduced by numbers and coalitions and where it is sensitive to external pressures. This sensitivity to external pressures may also lead to milder forms of surveillance and peer pressure in both regional and global forums.

As China's role in global economic governance evolves, it is expected to become more comfortable leading, coordinating, and investing in global public goods as it gains votes and voice in governance of the institutions. But there is also a chance that, as it gains more confidence, it will turn its back on the established institutions, instead favouring smaller networks in which it has more clout and where there are fewer perceived risks of containment. Which road it chooses depends in no small measure on how the bilateral relationship with Washington is managed and whether the two governments can overcome growing antagonism and mistrust. This priority is the subject of the next chapter.

7 The Inside Game

Mrs. Clinton said Beijing and Washington were trying to achieve something that has never been done. "We are trying to find a new answer to what happens when an established power and a rising power meet. We want a strong, prosperous and peaceful China."

– Kathrin Hille, *Financial Times*, 5 September 2012

Chinese state councillor Yang Jiechi stressed ... that China and the United States should enhance dialogue, mutual trust and cooperation and work together to build a cooperative partnership and explore a new type of inter-power relationship.

– *Xinhua*, 5 April 2013

The US-Chinese relationship is at a crossroads. As the former foreign ministers, Hillary Clinton and Yang Jiechi, have vowed, the rising power and established power can cooperate. Yet the relationship is clouded by foreign policy blunders in Asia on both sides and by rising tensions over cyber security. Until the announcement of the leaders' meeting in California in June 2013 there were troubling signs of drift. US hype collided with Chinese sensitivities to the United States' re-engagement in Asia, risking misunderstanding and miscalculation. No country would escape the effects of a confrontation between the two, but neither is conflict inevitable.

Nevertheless the relationship needs a reset. They could cooperate to move it onto a new trajectory, to "meet" and "explore." Cooperation on common interests in economic growth and political stability and on common strategic goals of non-proliferation, slowing climate change, and anti-terrorism could change the narrative of the relationship. In the period since the Second World War, the two have had episodes of intense military and ideological hostility – during the Korean and Vietnam wars, prior to the United States' recognition of the communist regime, and during the US-led embargo after the 1989 Tiananmen Square tragedy. Today, however, the two are deeply interdependent as barriers decline and trade, capital, people, and ideas flow between them.

Cooperation will take hard work. Long-term investments are needed to build mutual confidence and openness on which the trust is based. The framework for such cooperation was laid out in a joint statement by Presidents Hu Jintao and Barack Obama in January 2011, in which they "reaffirmed their commitment to building a positive, cooperative and comprehensive China-US relationship for the 21st century which serves the interests of the Chinese and American people and of the global community … based on mutual respect and mutual benefit in order to promote the common interests of both countries and to address the 21st century's opportunities and challenges."[1] The two leaders went on to specify a lengthy agenda to strengthen relations, promote high-level exchanges such as the Strategic and Economic Dialogue (S&ED), and address global and regional challenges. A year later, in a February 2012 visit to the United States, China's new president, Xi Jinping, stressed the importance of joint efforts to build mutual understanding and strategic trust, without which the two can achieve nothing. "China's rise is not the US's demise," he said.[2] Even so, tensions have been fed by standoffs in the South and East China seas, China's forbearance of North Korean belligerence, threats emanating from US presidential candidate Mitt Romney, a harsh report by the intelligence committee of the US House of Representatives, and ongoing tensions and differences over cyber security.[3]

MANAGING THE RELATIONSHIP

Each country fosters its own exceptionalist narrative, China its history, size, and successful re-emergence, and the United States its economic model, universal values, and military might. Since the Second World War, the United States has had alliances with Europe and Japan and shared memories of confronting a hostile Soviet Union. China lacks the experience of friendly allies – indeed, it claims to eschew alliances; its historical narrative is that of the superiority of the Middle Kingdom and of hostile foreign powers exploiting its internal conflicts and weaknesses in order to dominate it.

The speed with which China is now closing the gap in economic size is driving a wedge between the two countries, feeding both Chinese optimism about its superiority and US uncertainty about China's intentions and capabilities. In both countries influential groups forecast an inevitable contest for supremacy. Voices in the Chinese military and security establishments debate what China should do with its growing economic and military strength. Thinking in Marxist Cold War terms, they argue that China's foreign and military policies should focus on defining an enemy intent on undermining its core interests of security, sovereignty, and development – in other words, the United States, the declining hegemon that is expected to struggle to retain its power by containing China.[4] Others argue that China has outgrown the space afforded it in international governance institutions, which they regard as outdated and ineffective.[5]

In a thoughtful study, Kenneth Lieberthal, a Brookings Institution scholar, and Wang Jisi, Dean of the School of International Studies at Peking University, focus on the sources of this strategic distrust and ways to address them.[6] Wang argues that many Chinese see the US fondness for promoting democracy as intended to undermine China's leadership, and consider US arms sales to Taiwan and air and water-borne surveillance activities off China's coasts as provocative. Lieberthal counters that the US leadership is more positive towards the relationship than Chinese choose to recognize. The relationship with a rising China can be a constructive and cooperative one in which the two work together to address major global issues and reduce conflict. Although the mandates of their defence and security establishments are to anticipate threats, the lack of transparency on China's side about its military aspirations contributes to concerns that its policy is to undermine US interests, particularly in Asia.

Other US analysts are less sanguine than Lieberthal, with some political scientists painting particularly bleak pictures. One, based on the history and behaviour of regional hegemons, predicts that the United States will not tolerate China as a peer competitor, and that tension and conflict between the rising and established powers is inevitable.[7] Another asserts that China aims to project its military power and enforce its territorial claims for regional dominance, implying that the United States should increase its ability to cut Chinese supply lines, invest in undersea warfare technologies, and support the defensive capabilities of southeast Asian countries. Such analysts dismiss cooperation as "happy talk" likely to encourage Chinese hawks. They consider US re-engagement in Asia to lack substance beyond the Air-Sea Battle, a Pentagon term for a maritime strategy to counter China's growing capability to deny access to its waters, which implicitly encourages Chinese planners to test US capability and resolve.[8] Some argue that the United States should engage the Chinese in negotiations on serious limits, with the former drawing a firm line if necessary.[9] Others argue that, although the United States should support Asian neighbours' ability to withstand Chinese pressure, its military should increase interaction with its Chinese counterpart through exchanges and joint exercises.[10]

A number of senior US observers agree with former Singapore prime minister Lee Kwan Yew that "[c]ompetition between the United States and China is inevitable but conflict is not. This is not the Cold War ... China is acting purely in its own national interests. It is not interested in changing the world."[11] A more cooperative future is possible. Conflict is a choice, not a necessity. China is not an aggressor – its historical record is one of imperial expansion by osmosis rather than by conquest – and it now could not hope to conquer its neighbours. Furthermore, China's military buildup is unexceptional in light of its current economic resources.[12]

But China's rising global involvement is not without difficulties. Problematic is China's pursuit of its own interests seemingly with little regard for its effect on others. Chinese argue, however, that they have been careful not to undermine US core interests even though the US pivot has directly undermined some of theirs. Some see its behaviour as disruptive and as requiring a US response. They argue for changing the incentive structure in the bilateral relationship by creating a formal or informal "G2" partnership of equals whereby Chinese and US leaders together address global issues.[13] This, of course, assumes China will be content to work within the US-designed international system, and fails to take into account the reaction of powers such as Japan, the European Union, and India to being excluded from such leadership arrangements. A G2 would be possible only if the latter were unable to advance their own interests.[14]

IS A WIN-WIN FUTURE POSSIBLE?

These debates reflect fundamentally different assumptions: the military-security-intelligence communities assume a world in which the goal is supremacy with only one winner. The economic community assumes a world in which cooperation can lead to winning outcomes for both sides. Economic integration can be a brake on military aggression because of the costs of disrupting deep and extensive economic relationships. In Asia, however, deeper economic integration so far has failed to provide major impetus for cooperative regional security.

Can a mutually advantageous future be achieved? Those with experience managing the relationship see the answer as affirmative, but with caveats. First, as we saw in Chapter 6, in the global institutions China has yet to develop a view that is broader than advancing or defending its own interests, although Wang Jisi sees the outlines emerging of a more sophisticated grand Chinese strategy in which security is more broadly defined, relationships include participation in multilateral institutions, and the external effects of China's economic priorities receive more attention, as does the development of China's soft power, not least through commitments to transparency and accountability.[15]

Second, both the United States and China have major domestic policy preoccupations and challenges whose significance and call on political capital might be underestimated in zero-sum analyses. As Wang emphasizes, for China "[t]hese problems must be coped with seriously before we can really boast of being a first-class world power."[16] China is aging and still poor. Will its growing middle class become more outward-looking and supportive of the government's shouldering international responsibilities and burdens? The answer is unclear given the tendency to concentrate on Chinese interests. For its part, the United States faces the challenges of fiscal rebalancing, immigration reform, and infrastructure repair. Its leading military and security figures see the task of getting its fiscal house in order as a top national security priority – and one that encourages Chinese nationalist convictions that the United States' fiscal problems will deprive its military of the necessary resources to maintain its capabilities.

Third, mistakes and miscalculations are possible. These could come from the multiple fraught relationships in China's offshore waters, from a China convinced of US decline, and from US players who continue to think in terms of a US-led unipolar world. The risk, however, is that, with deep economic interdependence, unilateral punitive measures not only invite retaliation that damages the interests of both parties and innocent bystanders, but could spiral out of control into unintended conflict.

Deeper cooperation is possible, but it will need a push through the window of opportunity opened by fresh leadership mandates. A crisis, such as a natural disaster or a military miscalculation in the Asian maritime disputes, could force urgent cooperation. Bilateral cooperation is also more likely to deepen if Japan, India, and the European Union are preoccupied with their own domestic challenges. In the absence of such developments, more formal cooperation in leading the multilateral institutions makes sense.

AN AGENDA FOR DEEPER COOPERATION

An agenda for deeper cooperation should be based on two strategic principles. The first is recognition that neither can dominate the other. The second is that reducing mutual mistrust requires concerted high-level leadership. The 2011 joint statement by Presidents Hu and Obama implicitly observes these principles, setting the goal of a cooperative partnership that advances common interests, addresses shared concerns and international responsibilities, and specifies the principles of mutual respect and mutual benefit.

The coincidental timing of political cycles in the two countries opened the window of opportunity in 2012. Rarely are leaders in both countries available at the same time to make the necessary investments to move the relationship forward. President Nixon's 1972 visit was a major breakthrough, but it was not until 1989 that the two sides were ready to move forward again, and then the Tiananmen Square tragedy unexpectedly intervened. Domestic issues then became the focus on both sides until 1996, when a confrontation in the Taiwan Strait raised the costs of continued inaction. President Bill Clinton and President Jiang Zemin then committed to successive summits in 1997 (in Beijing) and 1998 (in Washington) to move things forward.[17]

A future agenda will have many elements, but two stand out: improving the inside game, or what the two governments should do in bilateral terms, and improving the outside game, which involves a wider set of players, including other countries and the countries' two publics, and which shapes opinion and perceptions of the relationship at home and abroad, beginning with Asia (I discuss the outside game in the next chapter).

Playing Elements of the Inside Game

The inside game begins with leaders setting directions and framing the relationship, and includes officials in both governments following through with efforts to build transparency, trust, and cooperation.

Convene Regular Meetings of Top Leaders

The two leaders meet several times each year on the margins of summits such as the Group-of-20, the United Nations, the Asia-Pacific Economic Cooperation forum, and the East Asia Summit.

These meetings, however, are scripted and rushed. In November 2012, during the Party Congress in Beijing, former US ambassador Jon Huntsman was asked by reporters for his advice on deepening bilateral cooperation. His top priority was for the two leaders to engage in regular, unscripted one-on-one meetings to set strategic priorities for the many facets of the relationship and to develop mutual confidence. Frequent re-evaluations and adjustments might be necessary at first, but eventually they would provide the parameters within which less formal interactions can take place to manage crises or misunderstandings.

The importance of the bilateral relationship needs to be reaffirmed, at a minimum building on the Washington visits of Hu Jintao and Xi Jinping in 2011 and 2012. At the time of writing in mid-2013, the informal two-day meeting in Sunnylands, California in early June 2013 suggested that leaders might be moving in the right direction. In the interim, they have relied on briefings by top officials and use of the telephone, reportedly to discuss cyber security and North Korea.

Increase Transparency, Particularly in the Military
The two countries' military relationship is the most urgently in need of engagement to build mutual confidence. The United States worries, despite China's public assurances to the contrary, that China seeks to dominate Asia and push it out. China's assertiveness in offshore maritime disputes and its willingness to link trade to disputes with Japan and the Philippines are worrisome indicators. On the Chinese side, public assertiveness by US military and security agencies in pursuing their mandates for threat identification and assessment feed mistrust, as does public rhetoric in electoral campaigns and US congressional committees. Such systemic and institutional roots of mistrust are difficult to change, but greater transparency can help.

US observers note that the Chinese military seems to be developing capabilities that specifically target US military platforms such as aircraft carriers and satellites. Both militaries are building their regional capabilities in Asia. Their ships and planes stalk each other. Some observers urge the two leaders and their militaries to discuss principles and ways to accommodate the interests of both sides, particularly on the potential flashpoints of Taiwan and North Korea.[18] Chairman of the Joint Chiefs of Staff, General Martin Dempsey, travelled to Beijing in early 2013 to explain the United States' defensive responses to North Korea's missile threats. China, however, did not explain its apparent reluctance to restrain such behaviour. Instead, it appeared to weigh its own interests in keeping the North Korean regime alive and the Korean peninsula divided as more important than the risks of outright nuclear aggression.

Deeper cooperation must begin at the top through leadership forums for discussion of strategic priorities, plans for exchanges and articulation of mutual expectations. These then open the way for cooperation at other levels where the two sides could build mutual confidence. Cooperation, which has already begun on counterpiracy, UN Peacekeeping and disaster relief could be expanded to other areas such as multilateral military exercises, maritime security, infectious disease controls and countering nuclear proliferation and terrorism.[19]

Deepen the Strategic and Economic Dialogue

The main channel for high-level bilateral consultation is the annual Strategic and Economic Dialogue, co-chaired by the US secretaries of state and the treasury and a Chinese vice premier and a state councillor. Venues alternate between Beijing (2012) and Washington (2013). Trade and investment issues, including intellectual property rights and trademark protection, government procurement, and barriers to investment and market access, as well as China's market-oriented economic reform agenda, apparently were discussed.[20] Former US secretary of state Hillary Clinton reported that the 2012 talks laid the groundwork for diplomatic coordination on security and proliferation issues and human rights, and established a Strategic Security Dialogue as a forum where military and civilian representatives can discuss such sensitive issues as cyber security and maritime security. The two sides also addressed cooperation on such global challenges as energy, the environment, development, and health issues.[21]

Several changes would add to the effectiveness of such forums. One is for the two countries' leaders or designated senior officials to manage the relationship on a day-to-day basis to ensure that the strategy moves forward. Students of the relationship note a strong correlation between forward movement and such management – and drift in its absence.[22] Singapore and Beijing already have such an arrangement in which Zhang Gaoli, a member of the seven-person Politburo Standing Committee, oversees the relationship as co-chair with a Singapore official of a leadership council.[23] As well, more effort is needed at operational levels to change attitudes and increase awareness of the difficulties of implementing principles agreed to at the top. Americans, in particular, need to develop a better understanding of why Beijing's policy commitments to protect intellectual property and expand government procurement to foreigners are not carried out at lower levels, where officials have conflicting priorities and incentives.

Future S&ED talks should discuss how to reconcile China's preference for an Asian free trade agreement and the United States' focus on the Trans-Pacific Partnership. Although the latter promises to restore declining US involvement in Asia's burgeoning trade and investment links, the goals and structure of the negotiations make it difficult for China to join. The objective rationale for this high-quality, comprehensive trade agreement is commendable, but it has become another factor feeding Chinese mistrust. Studies at both the official and non-governmental organization levels are needed to pave the way for the ultimate prize, a bilateral free trade agreement, by identifying bilateral economic complementarities and barriers that are potential issues for negotiation.[24]

Encourage More Direct Investment Flows
Two-way flows of trade, portfolio capital, direct investment, and people are already significant, but China's desire for access to US technology is a perennial sticking point. Looking to the future,

how can the two countries advance their economic relations in ways that help each to further its own economic goals?

Foreign direct investment (FDI) is the most promising channel. As flows increase, so will the number of stakeholders in each country who benefit from the linkages. In 2000 Chinese FDI inflows into the United States amounted to seven deals worth US$14 million; in 2012 there were sixty-two deals valued at US$6.5 billion, half of which was in the energy sector.[25] Like other foreign investors Chinese firms are attracted to the United States by the consumer market, the business environment, the work force, and the presence of strong competitive firms with global brands. Chinese enterprises are suspect, however, because of the absence of reciprocal market access, the lack of transparent corporate governance, and perceptions of government intervention in their decisions. Often overlooked is that Chinese investments have both preserved and created jobs: an estimated 27,000 to date, according to the Rhodium Group, which closely monitors Chinese investments. The Rhodium Group also estimates that, if the rapid rate of growth in Chinese acquisitions and investments continues, Chinese firms could employ between 200,000 and 400,000 Americans by 2020. Current trends also point to larger deals and increasing numbers of joint ventures, transactions in manufacturing, and strategic investments and co-financing deals in the energy industry.[26]

Certain transactions are politically sensitive on national security grounds, however, which raises questions about the potential for industrial fragmentation. Chinese demands for technology transfer as a condition for allowing US firms to enter its market are a long-standing example. The high-profile issues, however, are in telecommunications and information technology. In 2012 the US House of Representatives intelligence committee took this issue to an extreme when it investigated the Chinese firms Huawei and ZTE, two of the world's largest telecommunications equipment suppliers.[27] The committee criticized governance issues in the two firms and claimed to have evidence of espionage activities, although the Obama Administration attempted to downplay the committee's charges by stating that this "did not represent a final conclusion."

More effort is needed to educate Chinese companies about the US regulatory environment, factors that are likely to trigger a US national security review, and promising opportunities where Chinese investment would be welcome. For its part, the Chinese government should encourage "competitive neutrality" with respect to government financial and political support for state-owned enterprises. US pressure to improve the Chinese environment for innovation in a way that respects intellectual property rights would benefit innovation in both countries, allow more collaboration between Chinese and foreign companies, and build greater trust between them.[28]

Finally, to reduce barriers and help bolster confidence on both sides, the two governments should negotiate a bilateral investment treaty, as China and Canada have done and as the American Chamber of Commerce in China has suggested.[29]

Undertake Domestic Reforms as Fundamental to Mutual Respect
Domestic economic reforms are one of the foundation stones of mutual respect and bilateral cooperation. Each government needs to effect change at home to earn and maintain the other's respect. In re-establishing itself as a Great Power, China faces the dilemma that most threats to its political stability lie within its own borders, including struggles for autonomy in both Tibet and Xinjiang, human rights abuses, and popular demands to address economic inequality and for citizens to have more say about how the country is run. Leading Chinese thinkers admit that China has a bad international image – for example, pervasive corruption, environmental degradation, the lack of food security, and the seeking of asylum in foreign embassies by Chinese nationals – which can be addressed only at home through better interagency coordination, a more efficient and transparent government, more accountability, and stiffer penalties for corrupt behaviour. Success in implementing such reforms is key to China's ability to address global challenges, but, as with the economic rebalancing agenda, implementation requires political capital.[30]

For its part the United States must put its finances on a sustainable basis and reassure Chinese and other investors that it will not resort to inflating its way out of its problems. China's respect for the United States has declined as US economic performance has flagged and as Washington seems paralysed by political disagreement. Chinese ask how Americans can preach democracy abroad while apparently intent on undermining democratic practices at home, and they are puzzled that the US president seems powerless to implement his decisions on important issues.

Anticipate the Unexpected

Diplomacy will tend to the US-Chinese relationship day to day, do the hard work of drafting and negotiating the fine points of agreements, prepare and follow up high-level meetings, and is on the front line in times of crisis. Yet inescapable geopolitical complications arise, since the two countries are on opposite sides of the Pacific Ocean and the United States has long-standing military alliances with a number of China's neighbours. Diplomacy played a critical role in the North Korean crisis in April 2013, with visits to Beijing by Secretary of State John Kerry and US military and national security leaders to brief their Chinese counterparts on US plans to upgrade regional missile defence – which, of course, would be unnecessary if China were to rein in North Korea.[31]

There are other sources of risk as well. China risks hubris and miscalculation in the wake of the global financial crisis – many Chinese could be mistaken about the extent of the economic and political decline of the United States – so managing these risks implies a Chinese strategy of "integrating and hedging." For its part, as the United States takes an aggressive approach to rebalancing in Asia, it should be mindful of China's containment sensitivities and conduct diplomatic discussions of maritime regulations to ensure the free flow of energy supplies, help to develop domestic Chinese energy sources such as shale gas, and include China in regional military naval exercises.[32] In other words, the United States should make room for China, but set boundaries if necessary.

It is time now for China and the United States to replace crisis management through hurried diplomatic trips and telephone conversations with a thorough and thoughtful road map for developing a mutually beneficial relationship. Indeed, at the time of writing, there are encouraging signs that they are beginning to chart just such a strategic direction. As the bilateral relationship becomes global in scope, how can China and the United States work together? This "outside game" is the focus of the final substantive chapter.

8 The Outside Game

Work with China, don't contain it.

– Joseph S. Nye, Jr[1]

Xi is a leader the United States should seek to do business with, not just on the management of tactical issues of the day, but also on broader longer-term strategic questions.

– Kevin Rudd[2]

Managing the US-Chinese relationship for the benefit of both requires not just playing the "inside game" adroitly but also the "outside game" of relationships with other governments, both friendly and unfriendly, and with regional and global institutions. As the two giants intersect more frequently around the world, the set of players widens. Of most immediate and urgent concern is their relationship in Asia. Both have dominated the region at different times in history; both now should make room for the other and avoid reversing the remarkable post-war record of regional economic integration. The two have common global interests, and could produce key global public goods such as mitigating climate change and combatting cyber attacks, which US intelligence says has replaced terrorism as the greatest global threat.[3] The US and Chinese publics also have the ability to shape the relationship in important ways, through public opinion, cooperation, and exchange.

GETTING ASIA RIGHT

Getting Asia right is the top common priority of the two nations. Will each leave room for the other as they pursue their interests in the region? In China's geographic neighbourhood of east Asia, the tributary system once maintained extensive commercial and diplomatic links. In this context the United States is a relative newcomer, its maritime and diplomatic activity in the region dating back only to the middle of the nineteenth century. Then following Japan's defeat in 1945, the United States became the region's dominant power. The US-Japanese alliance's double guarantee that neither Japan nor China would attack the other provided political stability for the region's post-war economic miracle.

Looking ahead, Japan's wealth and technological superiority and India's economic emergence suggest that no one country will dominate Asia. The challenge now is to find ways to channel friendly rivalries into cooperative streams where everyone wins. The United States' engagement in Asia ebbed following the terrorist attacks of September 2001 as it turned its attention and resources to fighting terrorism in the Middle East and central Asia. Its recent re-engagement is now causing alarm, not only in China but also in other countries in the region that fear having to choose between the two if the United States should fail to follow through or its rivalry with China escalate. Many Chinese particularly resent that the United States believes it should have a voice in areas China considers its own core interest and in territorial issues it has with its neighbours.

The United States has three options, some have argued, to respond to China's rise: continue the status quo, withdraw from the region, or change its policy to share power with China – to accept China's Asian objectives as legitimate and strategic cooperation as key to maintaining regional stability. Australians, for example, have proposed a concert of the major powers, including the United States, to encourage China's regional participation rather than dominance.[4]

The region already has a number of institutions for economic and security cooperation organized around the Association of

Southeast Asian Nations (ASEAN), founded in 1967. To encourage participation among the large powers, ASEAN has pushed for economic and security forums with variable membership, sometimes including both Asians and Americans. Prominent among these are "ASEAN+" defence ministers' forums, trade agreements with each of the large powers, and the Chiang Mai Initiative emergency financing mechanism. Despite these initiatives, the region's security institutions face the complex challenge of managing China's boundary claims and its "coercive diplomacy."[5] In pursuing its core interests China has neglected to articulate broader goals that might serve its neighbours' interests. It has also permitted a plethora of players – the independent non-governmental International Crisis Group reckons as many as eleven, including provincial governments, state-owned enterprises, the navy, and the Fisheries Bureau – to pursue their own interests in the region with little coordination among them or with the foreign ministry. The People's Liberation Army, for example, has the same political rank as the State Council, the main organ of China's executive branch.[6]

In the past, governments in the region agreed to set aside maritime disputes and concentrate on long-term objectives. Now, competing claims in the South China Sea particularly involving China, Vietnam, and the Philippines, while subject to ASEAN's Declaration of Conduct, have defied bilateral resolution or the application of the global framework provided by the Law of the Sea Treaty. Among the solutions that have been suggested are government encouragement of commercial cooperation in energy exploration and development and the appointment of an "Eminent Persons Group" from nations with no claims in the disputes, who would be tasked to resolve conflicting claims in a manner similar to those with respect to Antarctica, where, for example, formulas have been worked out for dividing energy profits. In this regard, it has been observed that "30 percent of something is a lot better than 100 percent of nothing."[7]

Security expert Amitav Acharya argues that the existing paradigms for managing regional security cooperation all have weaknesses. Existing regional institutions have a competitive dimension, as China seeks to exclude other large powers while Japan and others support their inclusion. ASEAN, Japan, Russia, and India will oppose such suggestions as a concert of major powers or a "G2" consisting of the United States and China. ASEAN's proposal of a more deeply integrated East Asian Community is also moving slowly because of mistrust between Japan and China, not to mention the difficulties of defining the meaning of "Community."[8]

There is also a contradiction between the dangers of flashpoints in the East China Sea, North Korea, Taiwan, and, to some extent, the South China Sea, and the relatively weak institutional structures for managing security. ASEAN's vision of inclusiveness and open regionalism lacks the necessary cohesiveness and consensus to defend its members' collective interests. By default, but very conveniently for its own interests, the United States is expected to fill the vacuum by playing a counterbalancing role, at least until a regional institution becomes both credible and capable of doing so. One such candidate is the East Asian Summit, but it is one with its own problems.

The East Asian Summit

The East Asian Summit (EAS) began in 2005 with a leaders' meeting of the ASEAN+3 (ASEAN, China, Japan, and South Korea) and Australia and New Zealand. Since then India, Russia, and the United States have joined. The EAS is thus an evolving institution that organizers see as the kernel of a future East Asian Community. Although it is seen as having the potential to balance the security and economic interests of the region's major powers, its governance is problematic. The reality is Asian-style governance as seen in ASEAN, which prefers consultation, consensus, and practical problem solving to negotiation of long-term strategic goals. Appealing to the lowest common denominator, however, does not bring change.

As a leaders' summit, one would expect the agenda of the EAS to include both economic and security issues, yet the EAS has been almost irrelevant in managing tensions over China's maritime claims. Instead the Philippines looked to the ASEAN meetings hosted by Cambodia in 2012 as a venue for resolving its direct confrontation with Beijing, but there, too, the issues were not even on the agenda despite ASEAN's insistence on bloc negotiations with Beijing. ASEAN also pushed Beijing for a binding code of conduct.[9] Its inability to find compromise has undermined its credibility and potential for dealing with security issues, or to mediate disputes among its members. The merit of regular meetings of heads of government is indisputable, but surely their agendas should include discussions of pressing economic and security priorities, as well as the delegation of action to the appropriate implementing institution, as the G20 does.

Other ideas for the EAS include using forum meetings to organize "minilateral" dialogues to help manage the tensions of US-Chinese competition. The United States already holds regular dialogues with India and Japan, but all three have their own sensitive issues with China. Further regular three-way dialogues would be desirable, with the Americans and Chinese meeting with the Japanese and Indians, respectively, to help to bridge what could become major divides among the four.[10]

Free Trade Negotiations

Although the consensual style of diplomacy favoured by Asians makes it difficult to deal with security issues, trade agreements have become convenient instruments of friendly foreign policy. With the Doha Round of multilateral trade talks in limbo, Asia has seen a flurry of bilateral and regional trade-liberalizing initiatives, as discussed in Chapter 6. Some, such as the China-ASEAN Free Trade Agreement, are large pacts as measured by the number of countries involved – indeed, the overall value of the annual trade involved makes this the world's third-largest trading bloc.

Other regional trade negotiations are running along two potentially significant tracks, one organized around the United States and the other around China. The Trans-Pacific Partnership (TPP) track, which began in 2006 with four countries (Brunei, Chile, New Zealand, and Singapore), has expanded to include the United States and eleven other countries – most recently Japan

Figure 8.1. Asia's Trade "Tracks"

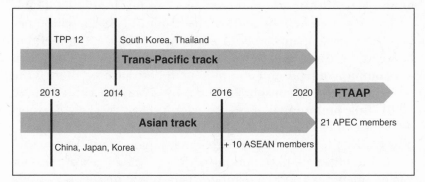

TPP 12: Australia, Brunei, Canada, Chile, Japan, Malaysia, Mexico, New Zealand, Peru, Singapore, the United States, and Vietnam; ASEAN membership: Brunei, Burma, Cambodia, Indonesia, Laos, Malaysia, the Philippines, Singapore, Thailand, and Vietnam.
Source: Adapted from Petri, Plummer, and Fan, *Trans-Pacific Partnership*.

– on both sides of the Pacific (see Figure 8.1). South Korea and Thailand are considering whether they will join, and the United States has said that China is free to apply, but it would need to be willing to discuss such features of its economic system as state-owned enterprises. The TPP is developing a negotiating template that addresses issues that hamper trade in global supply chains, including services trade and domestic policies towards competition, government procurement, and investment. It also aims to consolidate the expanding number of subregional agreements and their inconsistent rules of origin.

The other significant track is the Asian track, which reflects the ambition to negotiate an East Asian Free Trade Area among the ASEAN+3 – an elusive goal because each has its own agreement with ASEAN, but not with each other. More recently, these talks have been upstaged by an ASEAN proposal for a wider set of negotiations known as the Regional Comprehensive Economic Partnership, announced at the November 2012 EAS meeting, which would include the sixteen Asian members of the EAS, but not Russia or the United States, and which would aim to harmonize existing agreements.

There is an economic logic to these overlapping initiatives.

Successful completion of either would produce substantial economic benefits, since large economies are involved – the TPP is estimated to generate benefits of the order of US$295 billion per year for its participants on both sides of the Pacific.[11] Competition between the tracks also helps push both forward, with 2020 seen as a common milepost for completion. If both succeed there is the added incentive to consolidate them by giving the United States and China preferential access to each other's markets. Leaders of the member countries of the Asia Pacific Economic Cooperation (APEC) forum – including China, Japan, South Korea, and the United States – have endorsed a Free Trade Area of the Asia Pacific open to all APEC members. Consolidation seems possible since many countries are already members of both agreements.

One of the main differences between the two tracks is the "quality" of trade liberalization. In forming the TPP, its original members agreed on higher standards and a comprehensive framework as part of a long-term strategy to raise negotiating ambitions, to which the United States added its own agenda. With the bar apparently too high for China, one way to respond is to pursue only multilateral negotiations, but the complexities of getting such talks off the ground seem to be overwhelming: business communities are not enthusiastic and China has not provided any leadership. Thus, the most feasible alternative seems to be to move along parallel tracks. One suggestion is for China and the United States to include trade officials in their Strategic and Economic Dialogue to find ways to reduce the substantive differences between the trade tracks.[12]

The Asian track negotiations also differ from those of the TPP in their heavy focus on goods trade and reducing tariff barriers, some of which are still high. Their goal is to strengthen regional production networks for producing finished goods for export to Western markets, and negotiators are insisting on inclusiveness and tolerance for special sensitivities or interests. Non-tariff barriers are of less interest than they are to Western economies, which rely more heavily on services and investment and the protection of intellectual property. In their discussion of the TPP and Asia-Pacific integration, Petri, Plummer, and Fan suggest that, at the end of the day, the ideal template will offer market access for the manufacturing industries of emerging-market countries as well as good rules for the services, investment, and technology sectors of advanced countries. This is increasingly important in a setting where production systems are fragmented and span several types of activities and many countries; activities classified as services are often critical inputs in manufacturing, and vice versa. While Asian templates prepare the ground for greater cooperation by addressing primarily goods liberalization, US templates attempt to liberalize sectors that lead in both types of economies, ideally expanding opportunities for trade and production linkages among them.[13]

Getting Asia right is a central challenge and the stakes are high. China sees Asian relationships as central to its status and identity. The United States should respect such sensitivities by avoiding direct involvement in bilateral arguments and confrontations. Each government should also recognize the desirability of strong regional institutions to buffer and channel the inevitable rivalries, not just between China and the United States, but with Japan, Russia and India as well.

Strategies should also address China's conundrum in the TPP negotiations. TPP's future success is not assured as it is a complex negotiation with many participants. There are two big prizes in trans-Pacific trade liberalization: freer access for all to the two huge national markets and the associated momentum towards global liberalization talks that would be created. Thus, the preferred option is for China and the United States to work towards a free trade agreement that others can join. These negotiations would not be easy ones considering existing tensions over cyber security and differences over technology exports. But the preparatory studies would contribute significantly to the deeper mutual understanding necessary to deeper economic integration.

DEEPENING PUBLIC LINKAGES AND UNDERSTANDING

The second key aspect of playing the outside game is to encourage the deeper involvement of the US and Chinese publics and civil societies. Both governments need to find ways to change the suspicious public narratives that circulate in each country and to make their publics understand the importance of the bilateral relationship to their respective futures. President Xi Jinping seemed to understand this when, during his 2012 visit to Washington, he returned to the small Iowa town he had toured as a country official twenty-seven years earlier and stayed again with the same family that had hosted him then. Since he seems comfortable communicating with the Chinese public, he should find ways to inform it about the perspectives and responsibilities of China's being a global power.

State and provincial governors and municipal leaders in the two countries also should step up their collaboration by bringing together legislators, citizens, and students through twinning arrangements, tourism, citizens' forums and exchanges, scholarships, and media exchanges. Public sentiment needs to broaden beyond the narratives and preconceptions of the past. Both publics should learn to accept the other's system as it is and allow it to evolve. A more objective approach would reduce Chinese sensitivities that their core interests are threatened by moving closer to Americans. Such an approach is a fundamental building block of the East Asian Summit, whose members, the United States included, have signed a Treaty of Amity and Cooperation pledging non-interference in others' affairs.

THE JOINT PRODUCTION OF PUBLIC GOODS

The third dimension of the outside game is for China and the United States to work together on common global interests. Reports on the 2012 Security and Economic Dialogue provide insights into intergovernmental discussions on cooperation in addressing emerging global issues such as cyber security and producing the public goods required to address health, energy, environmental, and development issues.

Energy Security

For many years China was energy self-sufficient. Since 2007 China's energy policy has given increasing importance to energy conservation and innovation in renewable energy. Even so, 70 per cent of its energy requirements, particularly for electricity production and heating, are met from its own coal supplies. The rapid growth of its industrial machine as the world's manufacturing workshop now is feeding demand for oil, much of which must be imported through the world's busiest sea lanes. China worries about sabotage of those supply lines, recalling the US-led trade embargo prior to its recognizing the communist regime in 1972 that prevented China's access to foreign energy supplies and drove its quest for access to ports in the Indian Ocean and Arabian Sea.[14] At the same, the willingness of China's three large national petroleum enterprises to do business with rogue regimes has fed foreign mistrust even though all three are listed on the New York Stock Exchange and have shareholders. When they first emerged as players outside China, their intent was to tie up supplies for shipment to China; they now produce mostly for sale in world markets. With respect to improving international relationships, however, Beijing needs to encourage these companies to cooperate with foreign energy companies, to change the attitudes of its own policy makers, and to attempt to bridge mistrust about Chinese government intentions by becoming more involved in global energy bodies.

Climate Change

Nowhere is US-Chinese cooperation more desirable than in the global climate change negotiations, but providing joint leadership in global forums is problematic because of their differing views. In the United States, arguments rage mainly about the science. China's concerns come from a different perspective: it is a charter member of the UN Framework Convention on Climate Change, and sees itself as part of the developing world in divisions over negotiating the measurement and verification of emissions reductions. China and other developing countries view the negotiating approaches of developed countries as hypocritical finger pointing – especially at China, the largest emitter of CO_2 in absolute terms – even as they attempt to minimize their responsibility for reducing the stock of emissions already in the atmosphere. For this reason China is unwilling to enhance the concessions it has already made in the talks.

At the same time, China is making significant attempts to mitigate climate change with its unilateral targets to reduce CO_2 emissions and increase renewable energy in its primary energy mix. Its strategic emerging industries development plan envisages US$1 trillion of public and private investment over the next decade in "green" industries – renewable energy sources, energy conservation, and electric cars – and calls for energy prices to be determined more by market forces than by government fiat. China claims, and receives, little credit for such initiatives; it hesitates to lead because of its commitment to the coalition of developing countries in the climate change talks. Its detractors decry its reliance on industrial policies and criticize its cooperation with developing countries in undermining the creation of a global regime. Yet China's behaviour is reminiscent of the sometimes eccentric views of French leaders who push "French" perspectives and positions on international issues. In China's case such a stance puts the advanced industrial countries on notice that they cannot always expect to have things their way.

Cyber Security

In the climate change negotiations China is a participant, and to some extent a facilitator, but one willing to set limits based on its competing view of the burdens of responsibility for mitigation to be borne by advanced and emerging economies. Is this a precedent for its stance on producing other global public goods? Will it cooperate with the United States in such key areas that lack governance regimes, such as the militarization of outer space and cyber security? Recent public reports of the growth of cyber attacks are particularly troubling, implying a growing state of anarchy, spying, sabotage, and even warfare. China is described as engaging in extensive cyber hacking of personal accounts, penetration of other nations' critical computer systems, commercial espionage, and aggressive targeting of foreign corporations in China – indeed, some assert China to be the most aggressive cyber state in the world today.[15] Intense concern in the US Senate has led to the proposal of a bill, sponsored by Senators Carl Levin, John McCain, and others to require the director of national intelligence to develop and report a watch list of foreign countries engaging in "economic or industrial espionage in cyberspace" and directing the president to act on such reports by barring imports.

Cyber security is such a new issue on the global scene that no agreed governance framework – with norms, rules, and mechanisms for monitoring and enforcement – yet applies to it. It is an area where unilateral measures by either side to protect its population could be viewed as aimed at the other. Yet, like climate change, cyber security is a collective good: neither China nor the United States working on its own can produce a governance framework or monitor adherence to it. What is required is an international convention that includes a body of law to regulate cyber conflict and limit its effects. We are a long distance from that, but joint work to identify norms and rules would help reduce mistrust and head off mutually damaging conflict. Tackling such a collective issue together would have the added advantage of encouraging China's leaders to think and act in the larger global interest while serving the national interest without requiring major spending, which might be seen to detract from its rebalancing priorities and domestic demands for a social safety net.

In sum, in the outside game, China's newly assertive pursuit of its maritime boundary claims, the setting up of its own development bank, and its collaborating with other emerging economies on alternative negotiating approaches to climate change are signs that point to its engaging with the rest of the world as never before. The US-Chinese relationship is also globalizing as the two countries pursue their interests, but they are doing so in parallel, rather than in cooperative ways.[16] The relationship, therefore, is likely to become more adversarial. At one level this is normal. It would be unusual if the volume of economic exchange between the two countries did not cause competition and disputes, something with which Canadians and Americans are familiar from long experience with the world's largest trading relationship despite a common language and culture. China and the United States have deep differences, but they are also deeply interdependent, and the costs of the relationship's deteriorating into antagonism are high.

One route to a more promising future is for each to gain a deeper understanding of the other's goals and objectives. Working out mutually acceptable approaches to fraught issues – such as the futures of the Korean peninsula and Taiwan – and establishing a US-Chinese free trade agreement would set the regional relationship on a new trajectory and reduce the chances of an Asian "bloc" forming. Cooperating on new areas of common interest, such as a global cyber security regime, also would provide entirely new opportunities for these two deeply interdependent countries to enhance their relationship.

9 Partners and Rivals: The Uneasy Relationship

As the governments of China and the United States chart the course of the two countries' relationship in 2013 they will also be setting the direction for the next decade. They need to rise above myriad other distractions and think long term. Cooperation should become the relationship's *leitmotiv*.

Prior to the two-day working session of Presidents Barack Obama and Xi Jinping in June 2013, signals were mixed. Obama chose the Middle East as the destination of his first foreign travel since his re-election, pursuing elusive US goals for peace between negotiations at home to break the political paralysis in Washington over fiscal consolidation. New leader Xi's first travel abroad took him to Russia and Africa in pursuit of natural resources – admittedly a core Chinese interest – and to a summit of the BRICs (Brazil, Russia, India, and China) of possibly declining significance.

But these are early days in what is expected to be a ten-year Xi administration. His initial priorities have all been domestic: reining in wasteful privileged behaviour by officials, vowing to punish corruption, and advancing economic reforms. He has been silent on the intense debate about recognizing the constitutional rights of individuals, and instead of closing the hated labour re-education camps, he sent the issue for more study. At the same time, however, Premier Li Keqiang has proposed new policies to support private business and more market competition. Significantly, Xi's first foreign visitor, as he moved to calm tempers in the South China Sea, was the Sultan of Brunei, the 2013 chair of the Association of Southeast Asian Nations. The fate of the proposed domestic reforms will be clearer at the Party's October 2013 meeting. The central question is whether, despite a clear awareness that more domestic reforms are vital to the country's long-term interests, the Chinese leadership will fall short on execution, bringing about r-reform rather than R-Reform.[1]

A hypothetical dark scenario underlines the risks of drift in the relationship. Consistent with its containment obsession, China pushes the United States away from its borders at every opportunity. Its restraint towards the nuclear sabre rattling of North Korea's new leader is driven in large part by its determination to maintain the peninsula's division to prevent US forces arriving at its border. Suppose, in a disastrous miscalculation, North Korea launches a nuclear missile or experiences a nuclear accident causing devastating radiation and loss of life in South Korea and China's northeast. In the ensuing backlash, the United States might well attempt to organize China's neighbours into a counterweight, forcing them to choose. The responsibility would rest, not just on the Democratic People's Republic of Korea; China would suffer a grievous loss of reputation and trust around the world. Such a scenario is more than a flight of fancy. Strategic thinkers recall how a long period of relative peace in Europe was shattered by German unification in 1871. A militarization drive followed, threatening powerful neighbours that united to bring about Germany's eventual defeat. The German leadership failed to recognize that changing course could have established a new equilibrium and avoided conflict.[2]

The parallel today is the rising mistrust between China and the United States. China's leaders face serious challenges at home, while encouraging international footprints and seeking to repair relationships with neighbours after a series of foreign policy blunders. At the same time they risk getting caught up in historical narratives of vulnerability, mistrust of foreigners, and ambivalence about China's role in the world. Multiple pressures for and against domestic reforms and from assertive nationalists to stand up to the United States could distract them from acting in China's long-term interests as a mature global power.

This does not have to be the future, however; adroit playing of both the inside and outside games could prevent such a dangerous scenario. Carrying out this agenda will take hard work because partnership *and* rivalry are the reality. In the inside game the leaders of China and the United States should set the tone at the top by investing in regular one-on-one discussions of the strategic direction of the relationship and set the parameters for consultations and dialogues among their officials. Leaving such vital discussions to bilateral talks on the margins of international leaders' meetings is neither appropriate nor wise. The annual Strategic and Economic Dialogue needs to follow through more seriously on mutual commitments to cooperate. Military consultations should also occur on a regular, rather than an ad hoc, basis, with more transparency on strategies and goals. A *sine qua non* for mutual respect is domestic economic reforms to sustain growth and economic renewal in both countries.

Two desirable initiatives could set the economic relationship on a new trajectory, a bilateral investment treaty and a bilateral free trade agreement. In neither case would the negotiations be easy to conclude, but the necessary groundwork would deepen mutual understanding.

In the outside game the two giants are encountering each other more frequently around the world, but most importantly in Asia. Adding to the complexity of the game are Chinese historical geographical claims and the relationships both have with other countries in the region. Both should exert a restraining influence – China on North Korea and the United States on Japan. Both should seek common ground and principles for managing the future of the Korean peninsula as they have on Taiwan.

Both countries need to make new efforts to find space for each other in Asia. Both should take regional institutions more seriously, and to avoid splitting the region into blocs and forcing others to choose between them. Each should include the other in regional initiatives – China in regional trade-liberalizing negotiations and the United States in the Shanghai Cooperation Organization.

Beyond Asia, the two countries should seek common ground in more challenging areas than the easier targets of counterpiracy, disaster relief, and peacekeeping. They should develop common approaches to maritime rules, the protection of the sea lanes, and the production of global public goods such as governance regimes for mitigating climate change and averting mistrust and antagonism over cyber security. None of this, of course, will be possible without both high-level commitment and public support, and here both countries should seek innovative ways to broaden public exchanges and people-to-people linkages.

The United States and China are at a crossroads. It is in the interests of their neighbours and partners to encourage them to cooperate even as their tendency is to disagree. The health of this bilateral relationship is central to the collective futures of all of us. It is a complex relationship, not least because the two agree on so little, but also because the profound domestic challenges both countries face absorb large amounts of political capital. A credible foundation has now been laid for the two powers to "meet" and "explore" ways to avoid a downward spiral into competitive behaviour that benefits neither. Their leaders must use the opportunity now at hand to strengthen the pillars of the relationship – with realistic expectations, credible actions, and mutual respect – and build an enduring structure of cooperative relationships and institutions. The complex challenges of the twenty-first century demand nothing less.

Notes

Introduction

1 Graham Allison and Robert Blackwill, "Interview: Lee Kuan Yew on the Future of US-China Relations," *Atlantic*, 5 March 2013, available online at http://www.theatlantic.com/china/archive/2013/03/interview-lee-kuan-yew-on-the-future-of-us-china-relations/273657/.

2 "Special Report: America's Competitiveness," *Economist*, 16 March 2013.

3 At the 18th Party Congress, then-President Hu Jintao set a target of doubling per capita incomes by 2020.

4 For such an analysis, see Wendy Dobson, *Gravity Shift: How Asia's New Economic Powerhouses Will Shape the Twenty-First Century* (Toronto: University of Toronto Press, 2009).

5 Consumption as a share of GDP fell to an unprecedented 34 per cent in 2010; by comparison, in India the share was 54 per cent in 2007. See Michael Pettis, *The Great Rebalancing: Trade, Conflict, and the Perilous Road Ahead for the World Economy* (Princeton, NJ: Princeton University Press, 2013), 77. See also Nicholas R. Lardy, *Sustaining China's Economic Growth: After the Global Financial Crisis* (Washington, DC: Peterson Institute for International Economics, 2012).

6 The investment share of GDP soared from 35 per cent in 1990 to 50 per cent in 2010; see Lardy, *Sustaining China's Economic Growth*, 45–6.

7 See ibid., 62, for the evolution of China's national savings as a share of GDP. The ratio, averaged over 2007 and 2008, stood at 53 per cent. As every master's degree student of economics or business learns, in the balance-of-payments accounting identity, the trade balance is always equal to the difference between savings and investment.

8 Ezra F. Vogel, *Deng Xiaoping and the Transformation of China* (Cambridge, MA: Belknap Press, 2011), 664–90.

1 The Changing Shape of the World Economy

1 Allison and Blackwill, "Interview: Lee Kuan Yew."
2 International Monetary Fund, *World Economic Outlook* (Washington, DC: IMF, 2012), 101.
3 Dominic Wilson et al., "The BRICSs 10 Years on: Halfway through the Great Transformation," Global Economic Paper 208 (New York: Goldman Sachs, 2011), available online at https://360.gs.com. See also Conference Board, "Purchasing Power Parities and Size of GDP" (New York: Conference Board, 2010), available online at http://www.conference-board.org/attach/PurchasingPowerParities_GDP.pdf; and "Dating Game: When Will China Overtake America?" *Economist*, 16 December 2010, available online at http://www.economist.com/node/17733177.
4 Akiro Yashiro, "Human Capital in Japan's Demographic Transition," in *Human Capital Formation and Economic Growth in Asia and the Pacific*, ed. Wendy Dobson (London: Routledge, 2013).
5 See Charles Kindleberger, *Mania, Panics, and Crashes: A History of Financial Crises* (London: Macmillan, 1978). That book focuses on the Great Depression, but he works out his views on international cooperation in idem, *The International Economic Order: Essays on Financial Crisis and International Public Goods* (Cambridge, MA: MIT Press, 1988).
6 Author's interview with a Chinese economist from Tongji University, Shanghai, July 2012.
7 Loren Brandt, Debin Ma, and Thomas G. Rawski, "From Divergence to Convergence: Re-evaluating the History behind China's Economic Boom," *Journal of Economic Literature* (forthcoming).
8 David Dollar and Shang-Jin Wei, "Das (Wasted) Capital: Firm Ownership and Investment Efficiency in China," NBER Working Paper 13103 (Cambridge, MA: National Bureau of Economic Research, May 2007).
9 "China approves income plan as wealth divide poses risks," *Bloomberg News*, 5 February 2013, available online at http://www.bloomberg.com/news/2013-02-05/china-approves-income-plan-as-wealth-divide-poses-risks.html. Nicholas R. Lardy and Nicholas Borst report an unofficial household survey that finds the Gini ratio in 2010 to be 0.61; see "A Blueprint for Rebalancing the Chinese Economy," Policy Brief PB13-02 (Washington, DC: Peterson Institute for International Economics, 2013), 7.
10 These data are reported in "World Economy: For Richer, for Poorer," *Economist*, 13 October 2012, 4.
11 See Lardy, *Sustaining China's Economic Growth*, chap. 3.
12 Ibid., 73.
13 Ibid., 74.

14 See Gady Epstein, "Hung Verdict: Six Million Reasons to Pay Attention," *Economist*, 21 November 2012, 72.

15 See "Full Text of Hu Jintao's Work Report to 18th Party Congress," *Xinhuanet.com*, 17 November 2011, available online at http://news .xinhuanet.com/english/special/18cpcnc/2012-11/17/c_131981259.htm, accessed 20 November 2012.

16 "China confirms leadership change: full text of speech by new Communist Party General Secretary Xi Jinping at the Politburo Standing Committee Members' meeting with the press at the Great Hall of the People in Beijing," *BBC News*, 15 November 2012, available online at http://www.bbc .co.uk/news/world-asia-china-20338586.

17 World Bank and Development Research Center, *China 2030* (Washington, DC: World Bank, 2012).

18 Nicholas Borst, "China's New Income Inequality Plan," *China Economic Watch* (Peterson Institute for International Economics), 5 February 2013, available online at http://www.piie.com/blogs/china/?p=2285.

19 The value of total world goods trade in 2009 was US$25 trillion; see World Bank, *World Development Report* (Washington, DC: World Bank, 2012), annex table 5.

20 Ian Bremmer, *Every Nation for Itself: Winners and Losers in a G-Zero World* (New York: Penguin, 2012), 190.

2 China's Incomplete Transformation

1 Wang Tao, "China's Next Decade II: The Challenges of Aging," *Asian Economic Perspectives*, 7 June 2012, 8, available online at http://www.ubs.com/ economics, accessed 12 June 2012.

2 David E. Bloom, David Canning, and Pia N. Malaney, "Demographic Change and Economic Growth in Asia," *Population and Development Review* 26 (supplement, 2000): 257–90.

3 Because many Chinese women retire from active labour force participation while in their fifties and many men do so by age sixty, for the purposes of this study I define the active labour force to consist of the population between the ages of fifteen and fifty-nine.

4 See Wang Tao, "China's Next Decade II," 13.

5 Prominent advocates of this perspective include Cai Fang and Wang Mei-yan, "Growth and Structural Changes in Employment in Transition China," *Journal of Comparative Economics* 38, no. 1 (2010): 74–5.

6 See Zhu Xiaodong, "Understanding China's Growth: Past, Present, and Future," *Journal of Economic Perspectives* 26, no. 4 (2012): 121.

7 Nicholas Borst, "SOE Dividends and Economic Rebalancing," *China Eco-*

nomic Watch (Peterson Institute for International Economics), 11 May 2012, available online at http://www.piie.com/blogs/china?p+1258.

8 Zeng Yi, "Options for Fertility Policy Transition in China," *Population and Development Review* 33, no. 2 (2007): 215–46.

9 See for example, Gary S. Becker, "The Economic Way of Looking at Life," Nobel Lecture in Economics, 1992, available online at http://www.nobelprize.org/nobel_prizes/economics/laureates/1992/becker-lecture.html.

10 Guo Zhigang, "Too Few by Far," *China Economic Quarterly* 16, no. 2 (2012): 22–6.

11 Xing Yihang, "China to merge health ministry, family planning commission," *Xinhuanet.com*, 10 March 2013, available online at http://english.cri.cn/6909/2013/03/10/2724s752815.htm.

12 Wang Feng and Andrew Mason, "The Demographic Factor in China's Transition," in *China's Great Economic Transformation*, ed. Loren Brandt and Thomas G. Rawski (Cambridge: Cambridge University Press, 2008), 155–7.

13 See McKinsey Global Institute, "Preparing for China's Urban Billion" (n.p.: McKinsey & Company, 2009), 6, available online at http://www.mckinsey.com/insights/urbanization/preparing_for_urban_billion_in_china, accessed June 2012.

14 Ibid., 19–20.

15 Wang Tao, "China's Next Decade II," 23.

16 Mark MacKinnon, "China's 'left-behind children' an embarrassing side effect of rapid development," *Globe and Mail*, 17 January 2013.

17 World Bank and Development Research Center, *China 2030*, 365.

18 Ibid., 386.

19 Fan Gang, "The Megatrend of Urban," in *China at the Crossroads: Sustainability, Economy, Security, and Critical Issues for the 21st Century*, by Wang Jisi et al. (San Francisco: Long River Press, 2012), 25.

20 "University Exams: Fighting for Privilege," *Economist*, 3 November 2012, available online at http://www.economist.com/news/china/21565650-residents-clash-over-plans-let-children-migrants-sit-exams-capital-fighting.

21 World Bank, Commission on Growth and Development, *The Growth Report: Strategies for Sustained Growth and Inclusive Development* (Washington, DC: World Bank, 2008), 19–21, available online at http://www.growthcommission.org/indes.php?option+com_content&task+view&id+96&Item.

22 See Barry Eichengreen, Donghyun Park, and Kwanho Shin, "When Fast Growing Economies Slow Down: International Evidence and Implications for China," NBER Working Paper 16919 (Cambridge, MA: National Bureau

of Economic Research, 2011), available online at http://www.nber.org/papers/w16919, accessed July 2011.

23 Homi Kharas, "The Emerging Middle Class in Developing Countries," OECD Development Centre Working Paper 285 (Paris: Organisation for Economic Co-operation and Development, 2010), 31; and Elizabeth King and Emmanuel Jimenez, "The Skills of 'Tigers'," in *Human Capital Formation and Economic Growth in Asia and the Pacific*, ed. Wendy Dobson (London: Routledge, 2013).

24 See World Bank, Commission on Growth and Development, *Growth Report*, 21; and International Monetary Fund, "Brazil: Staff Report for the 2012 Article IV Consultation" (Washington, DC: IMF, 22 June 2012).

25 Kharas, "Emerging Middle Class in Developing Countries."

26 Author's interview with Fan Gang, Director, National Economic Research Institute, Beijing, in Toronto, 7 May 2013.

3 Turning Point or Countdown to Crisis?

1 Lardy, *Sustaining China's Economic Growth*, 54. This share compares with India's 54 per cent.

2 Ibid., chap. 3.

3 Mark Leonard, ed., *China 3.0* (London: European Council on Foreign Relations, 2012), available online at http://ecfr.eu/content/entry/china_3.0, accessed December 2012.

4 Ibid., 118–70.

5 See, for example, Douglass C. North, "Institutions," *Journal of Economic Perspectives* 5, no. 1 (1991): 95–112. Brandt, Ma, and Rawski, "From Divergence to Convergence," trace the roles of China's political and economic institutions in its economic performance since the Qing empire. They conclude with a series of questions about the current system's continued viability.

6 The data in the next two sections rely on Lardy, *Sustaining China's Economic Growth*, 68–112.

7 Ibid., 82.

8 Ibid., 71.

9 World Bank and Development Research Center, *China 2030*, 26. ·

10 Zhao Huanxin, "China names key industries for absolute state control," *China Daily*, 19 December 2006. The leading role was later stipulated as at least 50 per cent state ownership of a firm.

11 One study estimates SOEs and the enterprises directly controlled by them produce around 40 per cent of China's GDP. See Andrew Szamosszegi and Cole Kyle, "An Analysis of State-owned Enterprises and State Capitalism

in China" (Washington, DC: Capital Trade, 2011), 90, available online at http://origin.www.uscc.gov/sites/default/files/Research/10_26_11_CapitalTradeSOEStudy.pdf.

12 Yiping Huang and Bijun Wang, "Chinese Outward Direct Investment: Is There a China Model?" *China & World Economy* 19, no. 4 (2011): 1–21.

13 World Bank and Development Research Center, *China 2030*, 25.

14 Daniel Rosen, "China's 2015 Industry Consolidation Targets: Problem or Solution?" *China Economic Watch* (Peterson Institute for International Economics), 14 February 2013, available online at http://www.piie.com/blogs/china/?p=2303.

15 Ansuya Harjani, "Zombie firms a growing risk for China says Andy Xie," *CNBC Asia*, 29 August 2012.

16 See Pu Jun and Huo Kan, "Shining a Light on Too Big to Fail in China," *Caixin Online*, 13 August 2012, available online at http://www.marketwatch.com/Story/story/print?guid=7563DD88-E5AC-11E1-A54F-002.

17 World Bank and Development Research Center, *China 2030*, 27.

18 Ibid.

19 Alicia Garcia-Herrero and Daniel Santabarbara, "An Assessment of China's Banking System Reform," in *Who Will Provide the Next Financial Model?* ed. T.S. Kaji and E. Ogawa (Tokyo: Springer Japan, 2013), 154.

20 An estimate by Société Général, reported in "China slowdown stymies plan to curb shadow-banking risks," *Bloomberg News*, 17 July 2012.

21 For estimates, see Wang Tao, "Risks in China's Shadow Banking," *UBS Investment Research*, 16 October 2012; and David Barboza, "Loan practices of China's banks raising concern," *New York Times*, 2 July 2013, A1-3.

22 "China slowdown stymies plan to curb shadow-banking risks," *Bloomberg News*, 17 July 2012.

23 Chao Gupiao, "Capital Markets: The Light within the Gloom," *China Economic Quarterly* 16, no. 3 (2012): 15–16.

24 China, China Securities Regulatory Commission, *China Capital Markets Development Report 2008* (Beijing: CSRC, 2008).

25 Ibid., 289–90.

26 Lardy and Borst, "Blueprint for Rebalancing the Chinese Economy," 15.

27 Based on author's interviews in Chengdu and Luping during a research trip in November 2011.

28 World Bank and Development Research Center, *China 2030*, 32.

29 See, for example, Andy Xie, "The Only Way Out for China," *Caixin Online*, 13 August 2012, available online at http://www.marketwatch.com/Story/story/print?guid=B5371BDA=E5A9-11E1-A54F-002.

30 "Working the System," *Economist*, 29 September 2012, 49–50.

31 Xi Chen, "China: Two Faces of Protest," *Asia Pacific Memo* 183, 24 October 2012, available online at http://www.asiapacificmemo.ca/china-two-faces-of-social-protest.

32 This was reported by Jerome A. Cohen, "Courts with Chinese Characteristics," *Foreign Affairs*, 11 October 2012, available online at http://www.foreignaffairs.com/articles/138178/jerome-alan-cohen/courts-with-chinese-characteristics.

33 See, for example, comments by former US ambassador Jon Huntsman in Brookings Institution, "The Rule of Law in China: Prospects and Challenges" (proceedings of a conference, Washington, DC, 28 November 2012), 45–6, available online at http://www.brookings.edu/events/2012/11/28-china-law.

34 Miron Mushkat and Roda Mushkat, "Economic Growth, Democracy, the Rule of Law, and China's Future," *Fordham International Law Journal* 29, no. 1 (2005): 229–58.

35 Cohen, "Courts with Chinese Characteristics."

36 Available evidence indicates that "wealthy Chinese businessmen have been disinvesting and taking the money out of the country since 2010. One of the ways they can do that, without running afoul of capital restrictions, is by illegally under- or over-invoicing exports and imports"; see Michael Pettis, "Has the Great Rebalancing Already Started?" *Economonitor*, 17 August 2012.

37 Cheng Fashan, "More of Country's Rich Own Overseas Assets, Report Says," *Caixin Online*, 12 March 2013, available online at http://english.caixin.com/2013-03-12/100500565.html. This account reports a study by the Boston Consulting Group and the China Construction Bank.

38 "To Get Rich Is Not Always Glorious," *Economist*, 29 September 2012.

39 See "Zhou Qiang picked as head of China's Supreme Court," *Bloomberg News*, 15 March 2013, available online at http://www.bloomberg.com/news/2013-03-15/zhou-qiang-picked-as-president-of-china-s-supreme-people-s-court.html.

40 See Jerome Cohen's comments in Brookings Institution, "The Rule of Law in China: Prospects and Challenges," 53–4.

41 Randall Peerenboom, *China's Long March toward Rule of Law* (Cambridge: Cambridge University Press, 2002), chaps. 1, 10.

42 Cheng Li, "Introduction," in He Weifang, *In the Name of Justice: Striving for the Rule of Law in China*, (Washington, DC: Brookings Institution, 2012): xlvi.

43 Yu Keping, *Democracy Is a Good Thing* (Washington, DC: Brookings Institution, 2009), chap. 3.

44 Sun Liping, "The Wukan Model and China's Democratic Potential," in Leonard, *China 3.0*, 74–9.

45 Zhu Changzheng, "Closer Look: Divining Clues on the Future of Reform," *Caixin Online*, 9 May 2013, available online at http://english.caixing .com/2013/05/09/100525911.html.

46 Benigno S. Aquino III, "Inaugural Speech," Manila, 30 June 2010, available online at http://www.philstar.com/Article.aspx?articleid=589090.

47 See, for example, "Disclosing officials' assets," *China Daily*, 13 December 2012.

48 World Bank and Development Research Center, *China 2030*, 65–7.

49 Ibid. Other quick wins include abolishing secondary school fees in rural areas, changing local government growth targets to ones based on the quality of growth, raising energy, water, and carbon prices to reduce bottlenecks and shortages and encourage efficiency, and expanding public transportation.

50 See for example, "Getting Better," *Economist*, 27 October 2012, 69.

51 Evan Osnos, "Boss Rail: The Disaster that Exposed the Underside of the Boom," *New Yorker*, 22 October 2012.

52 Outlined in author's interview with officials of China's central bank, Beijing, November, 2012.

53 Mandiant, "APT1: Exposing One of China's Cyber Espionage Units" (Alexandria, VA: Mandiant, 2013), available online at http://intelreport.mandiant.com/Mandiant_APT1_Report.pdf.

54 Richard McGregor, "Chinese cyber spies mean business, says Pentagon," *Financial Times*, 10 May 2013.

55 David Barboza and Chris Buckley, "Beijing signals a shift on economic policy," *New York Times*, 24 May 2013.

4 China's Growing International Footprint

1 David Shambaugh, *China Goes Global: The Partial Power* (Oxford: Oxford University Press, 2013), 6.

2 "China eclipses US as biggest trading nation," *Bloomberg News*, 10 February 2013, available online at http://www.bloomberg.com/news/2013-02-09/china-passes-u-s-to-become-the-world-s-biggest-trading-nation.html.

3 Christopher Findlay, "Value-add data adds value to our understanding of Asia," *East Asia Forum*, 20 February 2013, available online at http://www .eastasiaforum.org/2013/02/20/value-add-data-adds-value-to-our-understanding-of-asia/.

4 See Loren Brandt and Eric Thun, "The Fight for the Middle: Upgrading,

Competition, and Industrial Development in China," *World Development* 38, no. 11 (2010): 1555–74.

5 Asian Regional Integration Center, available at http://aric.adb.org/ FTAbyCountryAll.php, accessed February 2013.

6 United Nations Conference on Trade and Development, *World Investment Report* (Geneva: UNCTAD, 2011), web table 4.

7 Daniel Rosen and Thilo Hanemann, *An American Open Door? Maximizing the Benefits of Chinese Foreign Direct Investment* (New York: Asia Society, May 2011), available online at http://www.AsiaSociety.org/ ChineseInvestment.

8 See Margaret Cornish, "Behaviour of Chinese SOEs: Implications for Investment and Cooperation in Canada" (Ottawa: Canadian Council of Chief Executives and Canadian International Council, February 2012).

9 Karl Sauvant, "Chinese Investment: New Kid on the Block Learning the Rules," *East Asia Forum*, 29 August 2012, available online at http://www .eastasiaforum.org/2012/08/29/chinese-investment-new-kid-on-the-block-learning-the-rules/.

10 Fu Jing, "Golden period for Chinese investment," *China Daily*, 29 September 2012.

11 Cai Xiao, "Outbound M&A activity mounts up," *China Daily*, 11 March 2013.

12 Huang and Wang, "Chinese Outward Direct Investment."

13 Szamosszegi and Kyle, "Analysis of State-owned Enterprises," 72–8.

14 Theodore H. Moran, "China's Strategy to Secure Natural Resources: Risks, Dangers and Opportunities," Policy Analyses in International Economics 92 (Washington, DC: Peterson Institute for International Economics, July 2010).

15 "Huawei corruption allegations given to FBI," *CBC News*, 10 October 2012, available online at http://www.cbc.ca/news/business/story/2012/10/10/ pol-huawei-information-turned-over-to-fbi.html.

16 SWIFT, "RMB Internationalization: Perspectives on the Future of RMB Clearing" (La Hulpe, Belgium: SWIFT, 29 October 2012), available online at http://www.swift.com/resources/documents/SWIFT_White_paper_ RMB_internationalisation_EN.pdf

17 Yu Yongding, "Revisiting the Internationalization of the Yuan," ADBI Working Paper 366 (Tokyo: Asian Development Bank Institute, July 2012).

18 Standard Chartered, "Singapore set to get a CNH boost," *Standard Chartered Global Research*, 21 February 2013, available online at https:// research.standardchartered.com/configuration/ROW%20Documents/ CNH_%E2%80%93_Singapore_set_to_get_a_CNH_boost_20_02_13_09_18 .pdf

19 World Bank and Development Research Center, *China 2030*, 39.
20 Jamil Anderlini, "Beijing confronts pollution dilemma," Financial Times, 14 January 2013, available online at http://www.ft.com/intl/cms/s/0/c673688c-5e2a-11e2-8780-00144feab49a.html.
21 The Twelfth Five-Year Plan's work plan on renewable energy, released in August 2012, includes a number of targets for 2015, including that renewables should supply 20 per cent of power generation and 9.5 per cent of consumption. These figures do not include nuclear power. Local officials will also be evaluated on meeting renewable energy targets.
22 Laurence Brahm, "China's Great Green Grid," *PacNet* 71A, 14 November 2012.
23 World Bank and Development Research Center, *China 2030*, 278.
24 Bonnie S. Glaser and Brittany Billingsley, "US-China Relations: Strains Increase amid Leadership Transitions," *Comparative Connections* (January 2013), available online at http://csis.org/files/publication/1203qus_china.pdf
25 International Crisis Group, "Stirring Up the South China Sea," Asia Report 223 (Brussels: International Crisis Group, 23 April 2012).

5 Twenty-First-Century Rivalry?

1 Kenneth Lieberthal and Wang Jisi, *Addressing US-China Strategic Distrust* (Washington, DC: Brookings Institution, 2012), 37.
2 David M. Lampton, *Same Bed, Different Dreams: Managing U.S.-China Relations, 1989–2000* (Berkeley: University of California Press, 2001); and Robert Zoellick, "Whither China: From Membership to Responsibility" (remarks to the National Committee on United States-China Relations, New York, DC, 21 September 2005), available online at http://www.ncuscr.org/files/2005Gala_RobertZoellick_Whither_China1.pdf, accessed 15 December 2012.
3 John King Fairbank, *China: A New History* (Cambridge, MA: Belknap Press of Harvard University Press, 1992), 137–9.
4 Ibid.
5 "China, Olympic Victim?" *Economist*, 18 August 2012.
6 China's external threats have been described as configured in four concentric rings, each farther away; see Andrew J. Nathan and Andrew Scobell, "How China Sees America," *Foreign Affairs* 91, no. 5 (2012): 32–47.
7 Insights based on author's discussions with Chinese economists, Cambridge, MA, and Toronto, May 2013.
8 Michael D. Swaine, "China's Assertive Behavior – Part One: On 'Core Inter-

ests'," *China Leadership Monitor* 34, Winter (2011), available online at http://media.hoover.org/sites/default/files/documents/CLM34MS.pdf.

9   "China officially labels Senkakus a 'core interest'," *Japan Times*, 27 April 2013, available online at http://www.japantimes.co.jp/new/2013/4/27/national/china-officially-labels-senkakus-a-core-interest/#.UYuwx19zbIU.

10   See Odd Arne Westad, "Memo to China: size isn't everything," *Bloomberg News*, 19 October 2012.

11   International Crisis Group, "Stirring Up the South China Sea."

12   The report of Dai's response is based on Acharya, "China's Rise and Asia's Security."

13   See Yan Xuetong, "The Weakening of the Unipolar Configuration," in Leonard, *China 3.0*, 112–17.

14   Nathan and Scobell, "How China Sees America," 35–7.

15   Linda Jakobson, "China's Foreign Policy Dilemma," *Analysis* (Lowy Institute for International Policy), February 2013, 6–7.

16   David M. Lampton, "China and the United States: Beyond Balance," *Asia Policy* 14 (July 2012): 21–49; Hugh White, *The China Choice: Why America Should Share Power* (Collingwood, Australia: Black Inc Books, 2012), Ibook location 1729.

17   Huang Jing, "China's Awkward Rise," *China Economic Quarterly* (March 2012).

18   Huang Jing, "China's Awkward Rise," 17–22.

19   Wang Yizhou, "Creative Involvement: A New Direction in Chinese Diplomacy," in Leonard, *China 3.0*.

20   Mark Leonard, "What Does the New China Think?" in Leonard, *China 3.0*, 23.

21   Aaron L. Friedberg, "Bucking Beijing: An Alternative US China Policy," *Foreign Affairs* 91, no. 5 (2012): 50–2.

22   Aaron L. Friedberg, *A Contest for Supremacy: China, America, and the Struggle for Mastery in Asia* (New York: W.W. Norton, 2011).

23   Zbigniew Brzezinski, *Strategic Vision: America and the Crisis of Global Power* (New York: Basic Books, 2012), Ibook location 2481.

24   Shambaugh, *China Goes Global*, 273.

25   "The Diversified Employment of China's Armed Forces," *Xinhuanet.com*, 16 April 2013, available online at http://news.xinhuanet.com/english/china/2013-04/16/c_132312681.htm.

26   Henry A. Kissinger, "The Future of US-China Relations," *Foreign Affairs* (March-April 2012), 44.

27   Robert A. Manning, "Beijing misreads US rebalancing in Asia," *Global Times* (Beijing), 7 February 2013.

28 Stephen Roach, "A nightmare scenario," *Caixin Online*, 20 August 2012, available online at http://english.caixin.com/2012-08-20/100426182.html.

29 Manning, "Beijing misreads."

30 C. Fred Bergsten and Joseph E. Gagnon, "Currency Manipulation, the US Economy, and the Global Economic Order," Policy Brief PB12-25 (Washington, DC: Peterson Institute for International Economics, December 2012).

31 James Clad, "Is China playing with American fire?" *Globalist*, 8 February 2013, available online at http://www.theglobalist.com/printStoryId .aspx?StoryId=9896.

32 Kissinger, "Future of US-China Relations," 44–55.

33 James B. Steinberg et al., "Turning to the Pacific: US Strategic Rebalancing toward Asia," *Asia Policy* 14 (July 2012): 21–49, available online at http:// nbr.org/publications/issue.aspx?id=263.

6 China and Global Governance

1 Jin Canrong, "China and the World in the Next Decade: Perspectives and International Politics," in Wang et al., *China at the Crossroads*, 45. This chapter draws on research in Wendy Dobson, "History Matters: China and Global Governance," in *China in the World Economy*, ed. Yiping Huang and M. Yue (London: Routledge, 2012); and Peter Petri and Wendy Dobson, "Asia in Global Economic Governance," in *Handbook of the Economics of the Pacific Rim*, ed. Inderjit N. Kaur and Nirvikar Singh (New York: Oxford University Press, 2013).

2 Petri and Dobson, "Asia in Global Governance."

3 To join the WTO thirty central ministries and departments were directed in 2002 to change 2,300 laws and regulations (eliminating many of them) and 100,000 local laws and regulations at the provincial and autonomous region levels; see Yu Keping, *Democracy Is a Good Thing*, 153.

4 Wang Hongying and James N. Rosenau, "China and Global Governance," *Asian Perspective* 33, no. 3 (2009): 5–39.

5 "Chinese President Calls for Joint Efforts to Promote Global Recovery," Xinhua, 28 June 2010, available online at http://news.xinhuanet.com/ english2010/China/2010-06-28c_13372324.htm.

6 Jamil Anderlini and Paul Betts, "China forced to put a value on its 'foreign friends'," *Financial Times*, 21 July 2010, available online at http://www .ft.com/intl/cms/s/0/eceb4a92-941b-11df-a3fe-00144feab49a .html#axzz2YZfS4FWf.

7 Yung Chul Park and I. Cheong, "The Proliferation of FTAs and Prospects for Trade Liberalization in East Asia," in *China, Asia and the New World*

Economy, ed. Barry Eichengreen, C. Wyplosz and Y.C. Park (Oxford: Oxford University Press, 2008).

8 Masahiro Kawai and Ganeshan Wignaraja, "Asian FTAs: Trends and Challenges," ADBI Working Paper 144 (Tokyo: Asian Development Bank Institute, August 2009), available online at http://www.adbi.org/working-paper/2009/08/04/3256.asian.fta.trends.challenges/.

9 This is not a necessary result, but appears to be the empirical implication of the nature of existing economic relationships and the proposed agreements; see Peter A. Petri, Michael G. Plummer, and Fan Zhai, *The Trans-Pacific Partnership and Asia-Pacific Integration: A Quantitative Assessment* (Washington, DC: Peterson Institute for International Economics, 2012).

10 Even so, small countries have repeatedly indicated they find Fund surveillance and advice helpful even though large countries have tended to ignore it.

11 Takatoshi Ito, "The Asian Currency Crisis and the International Monetary Fund, 10 Years Later: An Overview," *Asian Economic Policy Review* 21, no. 1 (2007): 16–49.

12 Edward M. Truman, "Sovereign Wealth Funds: The Need for Greater Transparency and Accountability," Policy Briefs in International Economics PB07-06 (Washington, DC: Peterson Institute for International Economics, 2007).

13 In April 2009 leaders authorized a one-time SDR allocation of US$250 billion and US$500 billion in new borrowing from Fund shareholders under the New Arrangements to Borrow. Japan and the European Union each agreed to lend US$100 billion and China indicated its willingness to provide US$40 billion in other ways.

14 Including the short-term liquidity facility, the flexible credit line facility, and the precautionary credit line.

15 This change in ranking depends on an overall change in financial contributions, including an increase for the United States. Congressional approval, however, has been delayed due to political gridlock, prompting outside calls for greater US cooperation; see "Reform the Fund," *Financial Times*, 11 March 2013, available online at http://www.ft.com/intl/cms/s/0/3e8ba820-8a4f-11e2-bf79-00144feabdc0.html#axzz2YZfS4FWf.

16 C. Fred Bergsten et al., *China's Rise: Challenges and Opportunities* (Washington, DC: Peterson Institute for International Economics, 2008).

17 Zhou Xiaochuan, "Reform the International Monetary System" (speech by the governor of the People's Bank of China, 23 March 2009), available online at http://www.bis.org/review/r090402c.pdf.

18 C. Fred Bergsten, "We should listen to Beijing's currency idea," *Financial Times*, 9 April 2009.

19 Details are part of a Strategic Partnership available from the Web site of the Association of Southeast Asian Nations, at http://www.asean.org/asean/ asean-summit/item/plan-of-action-to-implement-the-joint-declaration-on-asean-china-strategic-partnership-for-peace-and-prosperity-2011-2015.

7 The Inside Game

1 "Full Text of China-US Joint Statement," *Xinhuanet.com*, 19 January 2011, available online at http://news.xinhuanet.com/english2010/china/2011-01/20/c_13698492.htm.
2 Simultaneous translation available at http://www.youtube.com/ watch?v=ioEzUQFFH0s, accessed January 2013.
3 For a chronology and details see Glaser and Billingsley, "US-China Relations."
4 These views are reported and refuted by Wang Jisi, "China's Search for a Grand Strategy," *Foreign Affairs* 90, no. 2 (2011): 68–79.
5 Huang, "China's Awkward Rise," 17.
6 Lieberthal and Wang, *Addressing US-China Strategic Distrust.*
7 See, for example, John Mearsheimer, "China's Unpeaceful Rise," *Current History* 105, no. 690 (2006): 160–2.
8 Friedberg, *Contest for Supremacy.*
9 White, *China Choice.*
10 Stephan Frühling, "US strategy: between the 'pivot' and 'Air-Sea Battle'," *East Asian Forum*, 26 August 2012, available online at http://www .eastasiaforum.org/2012/08/26/us-strategy-between-the-pivot-and-air-sea-battle/.
11 Allison and Blackwill, "Interview."
12 Kissinger, "Future of US-Chinese Relations."
13 C. Fred Bergsten, "A Partnership of Equals," *Foreign Affairs* (July-August 2008), available online at http://www.foreignaffairs.com/author/c-fred-bergsten; see also Brzezinski, *Strategic Vision.*
14 Bremmer, *Every Nation for Itself.*
15 Wang Jisi, "China's Search for a Grand Strategy."
16 Koichi Kato, "Interview/Wang Jisi: China deserves more respect as a first-class power," *Asahi Shimbun*, 5 October 2012.
17 David M. Lampton, *Same Bed, Different Dreams*, 301–9.
18 Lieberthal and Wang, *Addressing US-China Strategic Distrust*, 44–5.
19 For more detailed suggestions, see Scott W. Harold, "Expanding Contacts to Enhance Durability: A Strategy for Improving US-China Military-to-Military

Relations," *Asia Policy* 16 (July 2013), available online at http://www.nbr
.org/publications/element.aspx?id=653.

20 See Timothy Geithner, Remarks at the Economic Track Opening Session
of the 2012 Strategic and Economic Dialogue, Beijing, 5 March 2012, available online at http://www.treasury.gov/press-center/press-releases/Pages/
tg1565.aspx.

21 See United States, Department of State, "The U.S.-China Strategic and
Economic Dialogue, Rounds I–IV Strategic Track Outcomes" (Washington, DC, 4 May 2012), available online at http://www.state.gov/r/pa/prs/
ps/2012/05/189288.htm.

22 David M. Lampton, "A New Type of Major-Power Relationship: Seeking a
Durable Foundation for US-China Ties," *Asia Policy* 16 (July 2013): 12.

23 See "Deputy Prime Minister Tharman meets top Chinese leader Zhang
Gaoli," *Straits Times*, 28 May 2013, available online at http://www
.straitstimes.com/breakingnews/asia/story/dpm-tharman-meets-top-
chinese-leader-zhang-gaoli-20130528.

24 For example, Canadian and Chinese officials completed a complementar-
ity study published in August 2012 of industries in the respective countries,
barriers to trade and investment, and potential negotiating issues; see
http://www.international.gc.ca/trade-agreements-accords-commerciaux/
agr-acc/china-chine/study-comp-etude.aspx.

25 As reported by China Investment Monitor, available online at http://rhg
.com/interactive/china-investment-monitor.

26 See Thilo Hanemann, "Chinese FDI in the United States: Q3 2012
Update" (New York: Rhodium Group, 18 October 2012), available online
at http://rhgroup.net/notes/chinese-fdi-in-the-united-states-q3-2012-
update

27 Ibid.

28 Suggestions put forward by Deputy Secretary of State Robert Hormats, "US-
China Economic Relations: The Next 40 Years," *Globalist*, 10 April 2012.

29 See Ted Dean, "Op-ed: The Right Time for a Bilateral Investment Treaty,"
AmCham China, 8 April 2013, available online at http://www.amchamchina
.org/article/11129.

30 Wang Jisi, "China's Grim International Environment," in Leonard, *China
3.0*, 121.

31 Mark Landler, "Detecting shift, US makes case to China on North Korea,"
New York Times, 5 April 2013.

32 Joseph S. Nye Jr, "Work with China, don't contain it," *New York Times*,
26 January 2013.

8 The Outside Game

1 Nye, "Work with China, don't contain it."
2 Kevin Rudd, "Beyond the Pivot: A New Road Map for U.S.-Chinese Relations," *Foreign Affairs* (March-April 2013), 12.
3 National Intelligence director James Clapper is reported to have made this assessment in a Senate committee hearing; see Pamela Dockins, "US ponders dealing with cyber attacks," *Voice of America News*, 19 March 2013, available online at http://www.voanews.com/articleprintview/1624832.html.
4 White, *China Choice*.
5 Bonnie S. Glaser, "China's Coercive Economic Diplomacy: A New and Worrying Trend" (Washington, DC: Center for Strategic and International Studies, 6 August 2012), available online at http://csis.org/print/38858.
6 "Vertical Meets Horizontal: Who Really Holds Power in China?" *Economist*, 1 December 2012, 50.
7 James Clad and Robert Manning, "What Roosevelt would do in the South China Sea," *Financial Times*, 4 September 2012, available online at http://www.ft.com/intl/cms/s/0/df61a7aa-f683-11e1-9dff-00144feabdc0.html#axzz2YZfS4FWf.
8 Acharya, "China's Rise and Asia's Security."
9 Greg Torode, "Islands row off the agenda at East Asian Summit," *South China Morning Post*, 21 November 2012.
10 Lieberthal and Wang, *Addressing US-China Strategic Distrust*, 48.
11 Petri, Plummer, and Fan, *Trans-Pacific Partnership*.
12 Ibid., 86.
13 Ibid., 14.
14 Zha Daojiong, "Energy Security: Just Like Everyone Else," *China Economic Quarterly* (March 2012): 28–33.
15 Shambaugh, *China Goes Global*, 297.
16 Pointed out in ibid., 75–6.

9 Partners and Rivals

1 For this useful summary expression, my thanks go to David Mulroney, former Canadian ambassador to China.
2 Henry Kissinger, *On China* (New York: Penguin, 2011), 514–21; and Edward Luttwak, *The Rise of China vs. the Logic of Strategy* (Cambridge, MA: Belknap Press, 2012), 56–65.

Bibliography

Acharya, Amitav. "China's Rise and Asia's Security: Towards a Consociational Regional Order." Unpublished manuscript, 2012.

Allison, Graham, and Robert Blackwill. "Interview: Lee Kuan Yew on the Future of U.S.-China Relations." *Atlantic*, 5 March 2013. Available online at http://www.theatlantic.com/china/archive/2013/03/interview-lee-kuan-yew-on-the-future-of-us-china-relations/273657/.

Anderlini, Jamil. "Beijing confronts pollution dilemma." *Financial Times*, 14 January 2013. Available online at http://www.ft.com/intl/cms/s/0/c673688c-5e2a-11e2-8780-00144feab49a.html.

Anderlini, Jamil, and Paul Betts. "China forced to put a value on its 'foreign friends'." *Financial Times*, 21 July 2010. Available online at http://www.ft.com/intl/cms/s/0/eceb4a92-941b-11df-a3fe-00144feab49a.html#axzz2YZfS4FWf.

Aquino III, Benigno S. "Inaugural Speech." Manila, 30 June 2010. Available online at http://www.philstar.com/Article.aspx?articleid=589090.

Barboza, David. "Loan practices of China's banks raising concern." *New York Times*, 2 July 2013, A1-3.

Barboza, David, and Chris Buckley. "Beijing signals a shift on economic policy." *New York Times*, 24 May 2013.

Becker, Gary S. "The Economic Way of Looking at Life." Nobel Lecture in Economics, 1992. Available online at http://www.nobelprize.org/nobel_prizes/economics/laureates/1992/becker-lecture.html.

Bergsten, C. Fred. "A Partnership of Equals." *Foreign Affairs* (July-August 2008). Available online at http://www.foreignaffairs.com/author/c-fred-bergsten.

Bergsten, C. Fred. "We should listen to Beijing's currency idea." *Financial Times*, 9 April 2009.

Bergsten, C. Fred, C. Freeman, N.R. Lardy, and D.J. Mitchell. *China's Rise: Chal-*

lenges and Opportunities. Washington, DC: Peterson Institute for International Economics, 2008.

Bergsten, C. Fred, and Joseph E. Gagnon. "Currency Manipulation, the US Economy and the Global Economic Order." Policy Brief PB12-25. Washington, DC: Peterson Institute for International Economics, December 2012.

Bloom, David E., David Canning, and Pia N. Malaney. "Demographic Change and Economic Growth in Asia." *Population and Development Review* 26 (supplement, 2000): 257–90.

Borst, Nicholas. "SOE Dividends and Economic Rebalancing." *China Economic Watch.* Washington, DC: Peterson Institute for International Economics, 11 May 2012. Available online at http://www.piie.com/blogs/china?p+1258.

Borst, Nicholas. "China's New Income Inequality Plan." *China Economic Watch* (Peterson Institute for International Economics), 5 February 2013. Available online at http://www.piie.com/blogs/china/?p=2285.

Brandt, Loren, Debin Ma, and Thomas G. Rawski. "From Divergence to Convergence: Re-evaluating the History behind China's Economic Boom." *Journal of Economic Literature,* forthcoming.

Brandt, Loren, and Eric Thun. "The Fight for the Middle: Upgrading, Competition, and Industrial Development in China." *World Development* 38, no. 11 (2010): 1555–74.

Bremmer, Ian, *Every Nation for Itself: Winners and Losers in a G-Zero World.* New York: Penguin, 2012.

Brookings Institution. "The Rule of Law in China: Prospects and Challenges." Proceedings of a conference, Washington, DC, 28 November 2012. Available online at http://www.brookings.edu/events/2012/11/28-china-law.

Brzezinski, Zbigniew. *Strategic Vision: America and the Crisis of Global Power.* New York: Basic Books, 2012.

Cai Fang, and Wang Meiyan. "Growth and Structural Changes in Employment in Transition China." *Journal of Comparative Economics* 38, no. 1 (2010): 71–81.

Cai Xiao. "Outbound M&A activity mounts up." *China Daily,* 11 March 2013.

Chao Gupiao. "Capital Markets: The Light within the Gloom." *China Economic Quarterly* 16, no. 3 (2012): 15–16.

Cheng Fashan. "More of Country's Rich Own Overseas Assets, Report Says." *Caixin Online,* 12 March 2013. Available online at http://english.caixin.com/2013-03-12/100500565.html.

Cheng Li. "Introduction." In *In the Name of Justice: Striving for the Rule of Law in China,* by He Weifang. Washington, DC: Brookings Institution, 2012.

China. China Securities Regulatory Commission. *China Capital Markets Development Report 2008.* Beijing: CSRC, 2008.

Clad, James. "Is China playing with American fire?" *Globalist*, 8 February 2013. Available online at http://www.theglobalist.com/printStoryId .aspx?StoryId=9896.

Clad, James, and Robert Manning. "What Roosevelt would do in the South China Sea." *Financial Times*, 4 September 2012. Available online at http:// www.ft.com/intl/cms/s/0/df61a7aa-f683-11e1-9dff-00144feabdc0 .html#axzz2YZfS4FWf.

Cohen, Jerome A. "Courts with Chinese Characteristics." *Foreign Affairs*, 11 October 2012. Available online at http://www.foreignaffairs.com/articles/ 138178/jerome-alan-cohen/courts-with-chinese-characteristics.

Conference Board. "Purchasing Power Parities and Size of GDP." New York: Conference Board, 2010. Available online at http://www.conference-board .org/attach/PurchasingPowerParities_GDP.pdf.

Cornish, Margaret. "Behaviour of Chinese SOEs: Implications for Investment and Cooperation in Canada." Ottawa: Canadian Council of Chief Executives and Canadian International Council, February 2012.

Dean, Ted. "Op-ed: The Right Time for a Bilateral Investment Treaty." *AmCham China*, 8 April 2013. Available online at http://www.amchamchina.org/ article/11129.

Dobson, Wendy, *Gravity Shift: How Asia's New Economic Powerhouses Will Shape the Twenty-First Century*. Toronto: University of Toronto Press, 2009.

Dobson, Wendy. "History Matters: China and Global Governance." In *China in the World Economy*, ed. Yiping Huang and M. Yue. London: Routledge, 2012.

Dockins, Pamela. "US ponders dealing with cyber attacks." *Voice of America News*, 19 March 2013. Available online at http://www.voanews.com/ articleprintview/1624832.html.

Dollar, David, and Shang-Jin Wei. "Das (Wasted) Capital: Firm Ownership and Investment Efficiency in China." NBER Working Paper 13103. Cambridge, MA: National Bureau of Economic Research, May 2007.

Eichengreen, Barry, Donghyun Park, and Kwanho Shin. "When Fast Growing Economies Slow Down: International Evidence and Implications for China." NBER Working Paper 16919. Cambridge, MA: National Bureau of Economic Research, 2011. Available online at http://www.nber.org/papers/w16919.

Epstein, Gady. "Hung Verdict: Six Million Reasons to Pay Attention." *Economist*, 21 November 2012.

Fairbank, John King. *China: A New History*. Cambridge, MA: Belknap Press, 1992.

Fan Gang. "The Megatrend of Urban." In *China at the Crossroads: Sustainability, Economy, Security and Critical Issues for the 21st Century*, by Wang Jisi et al. San Francisco: Long River Press, 2012.

Findlay, Christopher. "Value-add data adds value to our understanding of Asia." *East Asia Forum,* 20 February 2013. Available online at http://www.eastasiaforum.org/2013/02/20/value-add-data-adds-value-to-our-understanding-of-asia/.

Friedberg, Aaron L. *A Contest for Supremacy: China, America, and the Struggle for Mastery in Asia.* New York: W.W. Norton, 2011.

Friedberg, Aaron L. "Bucking Beijing: An Alternative US China Policy." *Foreign Affairs* 91, no. 5 (2012): 50–2.

Frühling, Stephan. "US strategy: between the 'pivot' and 'Air-Sea Battle'." *East Asian Forum,* 26 August 2012. Available online at http://www.eastasiaforum.org/2012/08/26/us-strategy-between-the-pivot-and-air-sea-battle/.

Fu Jing. "Golden period for Chinese investment." *China Daily,* 29 September 2012.

Garcia-Herrero, Alicia, and Daniel Santabarbara. "An Assessment of China's Banking System Reform." In *Who Will Provide the Next Financial Model?* ed. T.S. Kaji and E. Ogawa. Tokyo: Springer Japan, 2013.

Geithner, Timothy. Remarks at the Economic Track Opening Session of the 2012 Strategic and Economic Dialogue, Beijing, 5 March 2012. Available online at http://www.treasury.gov/press-center/press-releases/Pages/tg1565.aspx.

Glaser, Bonnie S. "China's Coercive Economic Diplomacy: A New and Worrying Trend." Washington, DC: Center for Strategic and International Studies, 6 August 2012. Available online at http://csis.org/print/38858.

Glaser, Bonnie S., and Brittany Billingsley. "US-China Relations: Strains Increase amid Leadership Transitions." *Comparative Connections,* January 2013. Available online at http://csis.org/files/publication/1203qus_china.pdf.

Guo Zhigang. "Too Few by Far." *China Economic Quarterly* 16, no. 2 (2012): 22–6.

Hanemann, Thilo. "Chinese FDI in the United States: Q3 2012 Update." New York: Rhodium Group, 18 October 2012. Available online at http://rhgroup.net/notes/chinese-fdi-in-the-united-states-q3-2012-update.

Harjani, Ansuya. "Zombie firms a growing risk for China says Andy Xie." *CNBC Asia,* 29 August 2012.

Harold, Scott W. "Expanding Contacts to Enhance Durability: A Strategy for Improving US-China Military-to-Military Relations." *Asia Policy* 16 (July 2013). Available online at http://www.nbr.org/publications/element.aspx?id=653.

Hormats, Robert. "US-China Economic Relations: The Next 40 Years." *Globalist,* 10 April 2012.

Huang Jing. "China's Awkward Rise." *China Economic Quarterly* (March 2012): 17–22.

Huang Yiping, and Bijun Wang. "Chinese Outward Direct Investment: Is There a China Model?" *China & World Economy* 19, no. 4 (2011): 1–21.

International Crisis Group. "Stirring Up the South China Sea." Asia Report 223. Brussels: International Crisis Group, 23 April 2012.

International Labour Organization. *Key Indicators of the Labour Market*. Geneva: ILO, annual. Available online at http://www.ilo.org/empelm/what/WCMS_114240/lang–en/index.htm.

International Monetary Fund. "Brazil: Staff Report for the 2012 Article IV Consultation." Washington, DC: IMF, 22 June 2012.

International Monetary Fund. *World Economic Outlook*. Washington, DC: IMF, 2012.

Ito, Takatoshi. "The Asian Currency Crisis and the International Monetary Fund, 10 Years Later: An Overview." *Asian Economic Policy Review* 21, no. 1 (2007): 16–49.

Jakobson, Linda. "China's Foreign Policy Dilemma." *Analysis,* Lowy Institute for International Policy, February 2013, 6–7.

Jin Canrong. "China and the World in the Next Decade: Perspectives and International Politics." In *China at the Crossroads: Sustainability, Economy, Security and Critical Issues for the 21st Century*, by Wang Jisi et al. San Francisco: Long River Press, 2012.

Kato, Koichi. "Interview/Wang Jisi: China deserves more respect as a first-class power." *Asahi Shimbun,* 5 October 2012.

Kawai, Masahiro, and Ganeshan Wignaraja. "Asian FTAs: Trends and Challenges." ADBI Working Paper 144. Tokyo: Asian Development Bank Institute, August 2009. Available online at http://www.adbi.org/working-paper/2009/08/04/3256.asian.fta.trends.challenges/.

Kharas, Homi. "The Emerging Middle Class in Developing Countries." OECD Development Centre Working Paper 285. Paris: Organisation for Economic Co-operation and Development, 2010.

Kindleberger, Charles. *Mania, Panics, and Crashes: A History of Financial Crises*. London: Macmillan, 1978.

Kindleberger, Charles. *The International Economic Order: Essays on Financial Crisis and International Public Goods*. Cambridge, MA: MIT Press, 1988.

King, Elizabeth, and Emmanuel Jimenez. "The Skills of 'Tigers'." In *Human Capital Formation and Economic Growth in Asia and the Pacific*, ed. Wendy Dobson. London: Routledge, 2013.

Kissinger, Henry. *On China*. New York: Penguin, 2011.

Kissinger, Henry A. "The Future of US-China Relations." *Foreign Affairs* (March-April 2012): 44–55.

Lampton, David M. *Same Bed, Different Dreams: Managing U.S.-China Relations, 1989–2000*. Berkeley: University of California Press, 2001.

Lampton, David M. *The Three Faces of Chinese Power: Might, Money, and Minds,* Berkeley: University of California Press, 2008.

Lampton, David M. "China and the United States: Beyond Balance." *Asia Policy* 14 (July 2012): 21–49.

Lampton, David M. "A New Type of Major-Power Relationship: Seeking a Durable Foundation for US-China Ties." *Asia Policy* 16 (July 2013).

Landler, Mark. "Detecting shift, US makes case to China on North Korea." *New York Times,* 5 April 2013.

Lardy, Nicholas R. *Sustaining China's Economic Growth after the Global Financial Crisis.* Washington, DC: Peterson Institute for International Economics, 2012.

Lardy, Nicholas R., and Nicholas Borst. "A Blueprint for Rebalancing the Chinese Economy." Policy Brief PB13-02. Washington, DC: Peterson Institute for International Economics, 2013.

Lee Jong-wha and Hong Kiseok. "Economic Growth in Asia: Determinants and Prospects." Economics Working Paper 220. Tokyo: Asian Development Bank, September 2010. Available online at http://www.adb.org/publications/economic-growth-asia-determinants-and-prospects.

Leonard, Mark, ed. *China 3.0.* London: European Council on Foreign Relations, 2012; available online at http://ecfr.eu/content/entry/china_3.0.

Leonard, Mark. "What Does the New China Think?" In *China 3.0,* ed. Mark Leonard. London: European Council on Foreign Relations, 2012. Available at http://ecfr.eu/content/entry/china_3.0.

Lieberthal, Kenneth, and Wang Jisi. *Addressing US-China Strategic Distrust.* Washington, DC: Brookings Institution, 2012.

Luttwack, Edward. *The Rise of China vs. the Logic of Strategy.* Cambridge, MA: Belknap Press, 2012.

MacKinnon, Mark. "China's 'left-behind children' an embarrassing side effect of rapid development." *Globe and Mail,* 17 January 2013.

Mandiant. "APT1: Exposing One of China's Cyber Espionage Units." Alexandria, VA: Mandiant, 2013. Available online at http://intelreport.mandiant.com/Mandiant_APT1_Report.pdf.

Manning, Robert A. "Beijing misreads US rebalancing in Asia." *Global Times* (Beijing), 7 February 2013.

McGregor, Richard. "Chinese cyber spies mean business, says Pentagon." *Financial Times,* 10 May 2013.

McKinsey Global Institute. "Preparing for China's Urban Billion." n.p.: McKinsey & Company, 2009; available online at http://www.mckinsey.com/insights/urbanization/preparing_for_urban_billion_in_china, accessed June 2012.

Mearsheimer, John. "China's Unpeaceful Rise." *Current History* 105, no. 690 (2006): 160–2.

Moran, Theodore H. "China's Strategy to Secure Natural Resources: Risks, Dangers, and Opportunities." Policy Analyses in International Economics 92. Washington, DC: Peterson Institute for International Economics, July 2010.

Mushkat, Miron, and Roda Mushkat. "Economic Growth, Democracy, the Rule of Law, and China's Future." *Fordham International Law Journal* 29, no. 1 (2005): 229–58.

Nathan, Andrew J., and Andrew Scobell. "How China Sees America." *Foreign Affairs* 91, no. 5 (2012): 32–47.

North, Douglass C. "Institutions." *Journal of Economic Perspectives* 5, no. 1 (1991): 95–112.

Nye Jr, Joseph S. "Work with China, don't contain it." *New York Times*, 26 January 2013.

Osnos, Evan. "Boss Rail: The Disaster that Exposed the Underside of the Boom." *New Yorker*, 22 October 2012.

Peerenboom, Randall. *China's Long March toward Rule of Law.* Cambridge: Cambridge University Press, 2002.

Petri, Peter, and Wendy Dobson. "Asia in Global Economic Governance." In *Handbook of the Economics of the Pacific Rim*, ed. Inderjit N. Kaur and Nirvikar Singh. New York: Oxford University Press, 2013.

Petri, Peter A., Michael G. Plummer, and Fan Zhai. *The Trans-Pacific Partnership and Asia-Pacific Integration: A Quantitative Assessment.* Washington, DC: Peterson Institute for International Economics, 2012.

Pettis, Michael. *The Great Rebalancing: Trade, Conflict, and the Perilous Road Ahead for the World Economy.* Princeton, NJ: Princeton University Press, 2013.

Pu Jun and Huo Kan. "Shining a light on too big to fail in China." *Caixin Online*, 13 August 2012. Available online at http://www.marketwatch.com/Story/story/print?guid=7563DD88-E5AC-11E1-A54F-002.

Roach, Stephen. "A nightmare scenario." *Caixin Online*, 20 August 2012. Available online at http://english.caixin.com/2012-08-20/100426182.html.

Rosen, Daniel. "China's 2015 Industry Consolidation Targets: Problem or Solution?" *China Economic Watch* (Peterson Institute for International Economics), 14 February 2013. Available online at http://www.piie.com/blogs/china/?p=2303.

Rosen, Daniel, and Thilo Hanemann. *An American Open Door? Maximizing the Benefits of Chinese Foreign Direct Investment.* New York: Asia Society, May 2011. Available online at http://www.AsiaSociety.org/ChineseInvestment.

Rudd, Kevin. "Beyond the Pivot: A New Road Map for U.S.-Chinese Relations." *Foreign Affairs* (March-April 2013).

Sauvant, Karl. "Chinese Investment: New Kid on the Block Learning the Rules." *East Asia Forum*, 29 August 2012. Available online at http://www.eastasiaforum.org/2012/08/29/chinese-investment-new-kid-on-the-block-learning-the-rules/.

Shambaugh, David. *China Goes Global: The Partial Power*. Oxford: Oxford University Press, 2013.

Standard Chartered. "Singapore set to get a CNH boost." *Standard Chartered Global Research*, 21 February 2013. Available online at https://research.standardchartered.com/configuration/ROW%20Documents/CNH_%E2%80%93_Singapore_set_to_get_a_CNH_boost_20_02_13_09_18.pdf.

Steinberg, James B., Thomas Fargo, Aaron L. Friedberg, J. Stapleton Roy, David M. Lampton and Wallace Gregson, "Turning to the Pacific: US Strategic Rebalancing toward Asia." *Asia Policy* 14 (July 2012): 21–49. Available online at http://nbr.org/publications/issue.aspx?id=263

Sun Liping. "The Wukan Model and China's Democratic Potential." In *China 3.0*, ed. Mark Leonard. London: European Council on Foreign Relations, 2012. Available at http://ecfr.eu/content/entry/china_3.0.

Swaine, Michael D. "China's Assertive Behavior – Part One: On 'Core Interests'." *China Leadership Monitor* 34, Winter (2011). Available online at http://media.hoover.org/sites/default/files/documents/CLM34MS.pdf.

SWIFT. "RMB Internationalization: Perspectives on the Future of RMB Clearing." La Hulpe, Belgium: SWIFT, 29 October 2012. Available online at http://www.swift.com/resources/documents/SWIFT_White_paper_RMB_internationalisation_EN.pdf.

Szamosszegi, Andrew, and Cole Kyle. "An Analysis of State-owned Enterprises and State Capitalism in China." Washington, DC: Capital Trade, 2011. Available online at http://origin.www.uscc.gov/sites/default/files/Research/10_26_11_CapitalTradeSOEStudy.pdf.

Torode, Greg. "Islands row off the agenda at East Asian Summit." *South China Morning Post*, 21 November 2012.

United Nations. Department of Economic and Social Affairs. Population Division. Population Estimates and Projections Section. "World Population Prospects, the 2012 Revision." New York: United Nations, 2012. Available online at http://esa.un.org/unpd/wpp/unpp/panel_indicators.htm.

United Nations Conference on Trade and Development. *World Investment Report*. Geneva: UNCTAD, 2011.

United States. Central Intelligence Agency. *The World Factbook*. Washington, DC: Central Intelligence Agency, 2012. Available online at https://www.cia.gov/library/publications/the-world-factbook/index.html.

United States. Department of State. "The U.S.-China Strategic and Economic Dialogue, Rounds I-IV Strategic Track Outcomes." Washington, DC, 4 May 2012. Available online at http://www.state.gov/r/pa/prs/ps/2012/05/189288.htm.

Vogel, Ezra R. *Deng Xiaoping and the Transformation of China.* Cambridge, MA: Belknap Press, 2011.

Wang Feng and Andrew Mason. "The Demographic Factor in China's Transition." In *China's Great Economic Transformation,* ed. Loren Brandt and Thomas G. Rawski. Cambridge: Cambridge University Press, 2008.

Wang Hongying and James N. Rosenau. "China and Global Governance." *Asian Perspective* 33, no. 3 (2009): 5–39.

Wang Jisi et al. *China at the Crossroads: Sustainability, Economy, Security, and Critical Issues for the 21st Century.* San Francisco: Long River Press, 2012.

Wang Jisi. "China's Search for a Grand Strategy." *Foreign Affairs* 90, no. 2 (2011): 68–79.

Wang Jisi. "China's Grim International Environment." In *China 3.0,* ed. Mark Leonard. London: European Council on Foreign Relations, 2012. Available at http://ecfr.eu/content/entry/china_3.0.

Wang Tao. "China's Next Decade II: The Challenges of Aging." *Asian Economic Perspectives,* 7 June 2012. Available online at http://www.ubs.com/economics.

Wang Tao. "Risks in China's Shadow Banking." *UBS Investment Research,* 16 October 2012.

Wang Yizhou. "Creative Involvement: A New Direction in Chinese Diplomacy." In *China 3.0,* ed. Mark Leonard. London: European Council on Foreign Relations, 2012. Available at http://ecfr.eu/content/entry/china_3.0.

Westad, Odd Arne. "Memo to China: size isn't everything." *Bloomberg News,* 19 October 2012.

White, Hugh. *The China Choice: Why America Should Share Power.* Collingwood, Australia: Black Inc Books, 2012.

Wilson, Dominic, Kamakshya Trivedi, Stacy Carlson, and José Ursúa. "The BRICSs 10 Years on: Halfway through the Great Transformation." Global Economic Paper 208. New York: Goldman Sachs, 2011. Available online at https://360.gs.com.

World Bank. Commission on Growth and Development. *The Growth Report: Strategies for Sustained Growth and Inclusive Development.* Washington, DC: World Bank, 2008. Available online at http://www.growthcommission.org/indes.php?option+com_content&task+view&id+96&Item.

World Bank. *World Development Report.* Washington, DC: World Bank, 2012.

World Bank and Development Research Center. *China 2030*. Washington, DC: World Bank, 2012.

Xi Chen. "China: Two Faces of Protest." *Asia Pacific Memo* 183, 24 October 2012. Available online at http://www.asiapacificmemo.ca/china-two-faces-of-social-protest.

Xie, Andy. "The only way out for China." *Caixin Online*, 13 August 2012. Available online at http://www.marketwatch.com/Story/story/print?guid=B5371BDA=E5A9-11E1-A54F-002.

Xing Yihang. "China to merge health ministry, family planning commission." *Xinhua*, 10 March 2013. Available online at http://english.cri.cn/6909/2013/03/10/2724s752815.htm.

Yan Xuetong. "The Weakening of the Unipolar Configuration." In *China 3.0*, ed. Mark Leonard. London: European Council on Foreign Relations, 2012. Available at http://ecfr.eu/content/entry/china_3.0.

Yashiro, Akiro. "Human Capital in Japan's Demographic Transition." In *Human Capital Formation and Economic Growth in Asia and the Pacific*, ed. Wendy Dobson. London: Routledge, 2013.

Yu Keping. *Democracy Is a Good Thing*. Washington, DC: Brookings Institution, 2009.

Yu Yongding. "Revisiting the Internationalization of the Yuan." ADBI Working Paper 366. Tokyo: Asian Development Bank Institute, July 2012.

Yung Chul Park and I. Cheong. "The Proliferation of FTAs and Prospects for Trade Liberalization in East Asia." In *China, Asia and the New World Economy*, ed. Barry Eichengreen, C. Wyplosz, and Y.C. Park. Oxford: Oxford University Press, 2008.

Zeng Yi. "Options for Fertility Policy Transition in China." *Population and Development Review* 33, no. 2 (2007): 215–46.

Zha Daojiong. "Energy Security: Just Like Everyone Else." *China Economic Quarterly* (March 2012): 28–33.

Zhao Huanxin. "China names key industries for absolute state control." *China Daily*, 19 December 2006.

Zhou Xiaochuan. "Reform the International Monetary System." Speech by the governor of the People's Bank of China, 23 March 2009. Available online at http://www.bis.org/review/r090402c.pdf.

Zhu Changzheng. "Closer look: divining clues on the future of reform." *Caixin Online*, 9 May 2013. Available online at http://english.caixing.com/2013/05/09/100525911.html.

Zhu Xiaodong. "Understanding China's Growth: Past, Present, and Future." *Journal of Economic Perspectives* 26, no. 4 (2012): 103–24.

Zoellick, Robert. "Whither China: From Membership to Responsibility." Remarks to the National Committee on United States-China Relations, New York, DC, 21 September 2005. Available online at http://www.ncuscr.org/files/2005Gala_RobertZoellick_Whither_China1.pdf.

Acknowledgments

This book was motivated by the opportunities for the US-Chinese relationship afforded by new leadership in Beijing and a fresh political mandate in Washington. Will the world's two largest economies compete or cooperate?

Economists assume the two can be partners – that their growing interdependence can mean mutual economic benefit and the production of global public goods of political stability and even a cleaner environment. Others, such as security analysts and political scientists, assume the two will be rivals – that they will follow other Great Power relationships in history that led to a winner and a loser. The two groups, it seems to me, should talk more to each other to develop a better lexicon for use in an integrated world in which shooting at one's competitor is likely to cause one to wound oneself as well.

Since 2009 the official language of Chinese and US leaders and their foreign ministers has changed as they have signalled their search for a new mode of cooperative interaction between the established and the rising power. Perceptions of global interdependence are behind this change. So is the recognition by both of the desirability of cooperating in this most important of external relationships as both face difficult and pressing issues at home. The United States' preoccupations are well known to Westerners; China's much less so.

When President Barack Obama was re-elected and President Xi Jinping selected within a week of each other in November 2012,

I was in Beijing. Chinese television screens were filled with interviews of Chinese and foreign guests in which the search was apparent for better understanding of two issues: what should be China's evolving role in the world, and what drives the interactions and policies of China and the United States. The mutual ignorance of the peoples of the two nations is obvious. In this book I hope to help Westerners understand China's strengths and weaknesses – those of the United States are all too transparent and familiar – and to frame these in the context of the leaders' strategic approaches to cooperation and competition. The reality is that they will be both partners and rivals: partners in addressing common collective concerns, and rivals in pursuing their own interests. Nowhere is this more apparent than in their evolving relationship in Asia and the Pacific.

Many people and organizations have been helpful to me in writing this book. I would like to thank colleagues at the University of Toronto, including Deans Roger Martin and Peter Pauly. At the University of Toronto Press, Jennifer DiDomenico has been consistently encouraging and insistent when necessary. Special thanks also go to research assistant Pranay Gupta and my very professional assistant Audrey Lake. Colleagues in my international networks have been valuable sources of insight. Collaborators include Peter Petri at Brandeis University, Peter Drysdale and Luke Hurst at Australian National University, Daniel Rosen at the Rhodium Group, and Fan Gang at the National Economic Research Institute in Beijing; members of the Pacific Trade and Development network, whose International Steering Committee I chair; Rod Hills, Zhang Liqing, Cheng Siwei, and participants in the International Finance Forum in Beijing; and other participants in both Harvard University's Asia Vision 21 and a Ditchley Park seminar in England. Fen Hampson of Carleton University, Jing Qian at the University of Victoria, colleagues at the Peterson Institute for International Economics, Loren Brandt and Zhou Xiaodong at the University of Toronto, Kevin Lynch and Neil Tait at BMO Financial Group, Margaret Cornish in Beijing and Mary Boyd at the Economist Intelligence Unit in Shanghai all willingly engaged with me on intellectual and political questions. Six reviewers –

former Canadian ambassador to China David Mulroney, Grant Reuber, Randy Spence, and three anonymous reviewers – also deserve special thanks for their helpful and insightful comments. The responsibility for the final product is, of course, mine alone.

This book builds on my 2009 study of China and India, *Gravity Shift: How Asia's New Economic Powerhouses Will Shape the Twenty-First Century*. I especially would like to thank Barry Norris, who edited both volumes and whose talented way with words shines through on every page.

Index

Acharya, Amitav, 136–7
aging population. *See* demographics;
 Japan
agrarian society: agricultural taxes,
 50; caregivers for the elderly, 36,
 39–40; infant mortality rates, 39;
 labour force, 36; social protests, 62,
 67; social safety net, 50. See also
 hukou; land; rural-urban migration
Ai Weiwei, 27
APEC (Asia-Pacific Economic Cooperation), 110, 139f, 140
Apple, supply chain, 74–5, 80
ASEAN (Association of Southeast
 Asian Nations): boundary dispute
 negotiations, 89, 93, 136–8; China's
 global governance objectives, 108t;
 China's objectives, 75, 110; currency regionalization, 84; currency
 swap agreements, 114; development fund, 116; emergency financing (CMIM), 108t, 114, 115, 136;
 members, 75, 110, 136; trade agreements, 138–40, 139f
ASEAN-China Investment Cooperation Fund, 116

Asian Development Bank, 82, 108t,
 116
Asia-Pacific region: dominance of
 India, Japan, or China, 135; fear
 of US-China rivalry, 135; growth in
 GDP (2005–30), 104f; US involvement, 14, 93–4, 123, 135–6. *See
 also* India; international relations,
 China; Japan; "outside game"
Australia: ASEAN member, 110;
 China's foreign investment in,
 111; EAS member, 137–8; Obama's
 speech to parliament, 94–5; proposal for cooperation, 135; trade
 with China, 30, 30t, 76; US security
 alliance, 92
auto sector: electric cars, 144; emerging industries, 71, 75; fuel prices,
 50; ownership comparisons, 20t,
 32, 62; SOE industries, 52
aviation, as SOE sector, 52, 71

banking system: auditing and accounting standards, 57, 68; bad
 loans, 54–5; Bank of China, 19, 83;
 and capital outflow, 65, 157n36;

development banks, 53, 108t, 116–17; ease of doing business, 70–1; global governance objectives, 108t; government role, 54–5; interest-rate deregulation, 26, 29, 57, 70; interest rates on savings, 26, 29, 48, 50, 54, 55; interest subsidies for SOEs, 24, 25; and international investment, 82; reforms proposed, 54–6, 57; regulation of, 54, 115–16; risk management, 55; shadow banking, 51, 55–6; and stock markets, 55; subsidized loans to SOEs, 24, 25, 53. *See also* Asian Development Bank; financial system, China; savings; World Bank

Beijing, pollution, 86–7

bond markets, China: absence of efficient markets, 54, 84; bonds for small business lending, 56; corporate SOE bonds, 57; municipal bonds, 42, 60; non-state enterprise bonds, 57; "panda" and "dim sum" bonds, 82–3; reforms proposed, 57–8, 60; regional markets, 82; value of bonds, 57. *See also* financial markets, China

borrowing. *See* banking system; financial system

Borst, Nicholas, 152n9, 156n26

boundary claims: ASEAN response to, 89, 136; China's sense of vulnerability, 92; Diaoyu/Senkaku dispute, 87–8, 93, 161n9; miscalculations, 88, 99, 119; proposed solutions, 136; South China Sea, 87–9, 93, 101, 105, 136; US-China relations, 14, 89, 93–4, 127–8, 137

Bo Xilai, 64, 65, 69

Brazil: BRIC dialogues, 101, 109, 147;

environmental agreement, 117; income inequality, 25, 45; middle-income trap, 44, 45–6; spending as per cent of GDP (2013), 24; trade with China, 30, 30t

bribery. *See* corruption

BRIC dialogues, 101, 109, 147

Brunei as TPP member, 97, 138–9

bureaucracy, Party. *See* Communist Party of China

Bush, George W., administration, 97

Cambodia, productivity, 38f

Canada: APEC member, 110; global stock holdings, 76, 76f; trade, 30, 30t; trade and investment agreement with China, 131, 165n24

capital markets, 56–8, 82. *See also* bond markets, China; financial markets, China

carbon dioxide emissions, 19, 20t, 118, 143–4. *See also* environment

Central Commission for Discipline Inspection, 28, 66, 69

Central Commission of Politics and Law, 65–6

Central Committee, 65

Central Organization Department, 11–12, 79

Chengdu, Sichuan: *hukou* reforms, 43; land reform, 59–60

Chen Yibing, 92

Chiang Mai Initiative (CMIM), 108t, 114, 115, 136

children. *See* families

Chile as TPP member, 97, 138–9

China 2030, 28–9, 47, 70

China Banking Regulatory Commission, 54

China Development Bank, 53

China Investment Corporation, 116
Chinalco, 111
China National Offshore Oil Corporation, 52
China Securities Regulatory Commission, 56–7
Chongquing, reforms, 43, 59
cities. *See* urban areas
clan relationships. See *guanxi* networks
climate change: China's global governance objectives, 108t, 117–18, 143–4. *See also* environment
Clinton, Bill, 126
Clinton, Hillary, 100, 120, 128
CNOOC (China National Offshore Oil Corp.), 77–8, 79, 111
coal, 25, 51, 52, 86, 117, 143
communes ("iron rice bowl"), 36, 48
Communist Party of China: authoritarianism, 11; bureaucracy, 24, 32; Congress meetings, 27, 29, 39, 62, 64, 65, 66, 72; corruption, 10–11, 27–8, 32, 61, 64; disclosure of personal assets, 69; and economic growth, 24; and elections, 62; *guanxi* networks, 12, 28, 32–3, 64; history of, 12–13; leadership expertise, 11–12, 32–3; leadership in reform movements, 69–70; leadership privileges, 68–9; and legal system, 10–11, 63–7; legitimization through economic growth, 4, 9, 11, 61; reforms proposed, 11, 13, 27–9, 66–72, 148; and social protests, 11, 61–2, 64, 67; and SOEs, 13, 24, 54. *See also* state-owned enterprises (SOEs); Xi Jinping
competition: and state control, 10
Confucian tradition, 12–13, 63

consumers and consumption: comparison of China and US, 20t; domestic demand, 26, 47, 62; and economic restructuring, 46, 48; household consumption as per cent of GDP (2013), 24; and interest rates on savings, 50; producers favoured over consumers, 24, 47; and urban growth, 41; vehicle ownership, 19, 20t. *See also* middle class
cooperation, China and US: channels for, 6; and crises, 125; domestic challenges, 6, 9, 124–5; economic interdependence, 6, 99–102, 125; leadership by Xi and Obama, 15–16; mutual need for, 6, 120–1; use of "inside game" and "outside game," 15. *See also* "inside game"; international relations, China and US; "outside game"
Copenhagen Conference, 117
corruption: bribery, 62; and capital outflow, 65, 157n36; and ease of doing business, 70; in elections, 62; and employment, 11, 61; and *guanxi* networks, 12, 64; land sales, 58; and legal system, 10–11, 64; and Party, 10–11, 27–8, 61, 64; public criticism of, 27; reforms, 11, 70; rent-seeking behaviour, 10–11, 61, 70
crisis in 2008-09, financial. *See* recession of 2008–09
currency, China (RMB): black markets, 61; and capital outflow, 65, 157n36; currency swaps, 83; exchange rate and US dollar valuation, 114; exchange-rate appreciation, 48; exchange-rate criticism by G20, 107; exchange-rate flex-

ibility, 26, 57, 70, 83–4, 113; goals
in Twelfth Five-Year Plan, 115;
international use, 73, 80–2, 83–4;
market volatility, 80, 82; reforms
proposed, 80, 83–5; regionalization
of, 58, 82–4; and restricted capital
accounts, 58; Romney on currency
manipulation, 97–8, 99; undervalu-
ation, 9, 45, 74, 80, 98–9, 114. *See
also* trade, China
currency, US: China's foreign-
exchange reserves (2005–12), 19,
30–2, 31t, 114; China's holdings of
US treasury bonds (2001–13), 31f;
impact of 2008 recession, 31; international use, 80–2, 83–4, 113–14;
oil exports, 82
cyber security: attacks as global
threat, 134, 144–5; breaches and
US-China relations, 4, 72, 85,
144–5; and free trade negotiations,
141; host country concerns, 78; and
public engagement, 15; Strategic
and Economic Dialogue, 128–9;
US-China cooperation, 145, 146

Dai Bingguo, 93–4
demographics: demographic
dividend, 34–5, 36; demographic
pyramid, 7; dependency ratio and
population growth, 34–7, 35f; infant mortality rates, 39; one-child
policy, 34, 37–8, 39–40; population,
20t, 40–1, 41f; sex ratio, 39–40. *See
also* families
Dempsey, Martin, 128
Deng Xiaoping, 10, 48, 63, 95, 101
development banks, 53, 108t, 116–17.
See also Asian Development Bank;
China Development Bank

Diaoyu/Senkaku dispute. *See* boundary claims
dipiao land trading system, 59–60. *See
also* land
Dobson, Wendy, 108t, 151n4,
162nn1–2
Doha Round, 107, 138
Durban Conference, 117

earthquake (2008), China, 59–60
EAS (East Asia Summit), 97, 137–8,
139, 142
East Asia Free Trade Area, 139
East Asia Pacific, productivity, 38f
East China Sea dispute. *See* boundary
claims
economy, China: capital outflow, 65,
78, 157n36; comparison with US
(2013), 32; domestic demand, 26,
47, 62, 125; global role in stabilization, 21–3; growth-accounting
framework, 8–9; holdings of US
treasury bonds, 31f; *hukou* reform,
8, 29; integration with world
economy, 73–4; per capita income
and spending (2013), 24; producers favoured over consumers, 24,
47; reforms, 24, 26–9, 131; regional
differences, 9. *See also* consumers
and consumption; economy, China,
growth; income; interdependence
economy, China, growth: comparative
growth, 22f, 32; demographic dividend, 34–5, 36; future trends, 21–2;
GDP comparisons, 18t; growth-
accounting framework, 8–9; growth
in GDP (2005–30), 104f; growth
rate, 17, 37; impact of 2008-09 recession, 17, 18t, 21; middle-income
trap and stagnation, 6, 44–6; pro-

ductivity (1990–2010), 37–8, 38f; reforms, 37–8, 41–3, 47–9, 67–8; and urbanization, 40–2, 41f; Wen's views (2007), 8, 47

economy, US: China's foreign direct investment, 130; China's holdings of US treasury bonds, 30–2, 31f; comparative growth, 22f; future trends, 21–2; GDP comparisons, 18t; global stock holdings, 76f; growth in GDP (2005–30), 104f; growth rate (2013), 21; history of transitions, 22–3; income inequality, 25; per capita spending as per cent of GDP (2013), 24; reforms proposed, 132. See also currency, US; military, US; recession of 2008–09; trade, US

education: and economic restructuring, 26–7, 29, 46; education abroad, 65; gaokao (college entrance exams), 43; goals in Twelfth Five-Year Plan, 40; impact of hukou on, 25, 42, 43; increased spending, 50; and labour force, 40; legal education, 63, 64; rural students, 26, 29, 50, 158n49

Eichengreen, Barry, 44, 45

electricity, 51, 53, 87, 143

employment: corruption and hiring, 11, 61; and economic restructuring, 26; employment in agriculture, 36–7; favouritism and connections, 61; impact of hukou on, 25; middle-income trap, 44–5; in SOEs, 52–3, 79; unemployment, 25, 40, 53; unemployment benefits, 50; in urban areas, 41; in US from foreign investment, 130. See also labour force

energy, China: electricity, 51, 53, 87, 143; emerging green industries, 71, 118, 144; energy security, 142–3; foreign investment, 78–9, 143; goals in Twelfth Five-Year Plan, 87, 160n21; government role, 50–1, 52, 86; in growth-accounting framework, 8; oil and gas, 25, 50, 52, 143; power generation, 52, 160n21; prices, 24, 25, 50–1, 86, 144; private ownership, 72; reforms, 143–4; renewable energy, 86, 118, 144, 160n21; solar energy, 53, 86, 118; US-China relations, 132. See also CNOOC; coal; environment

energy, US: China's foreign direct investment, 130; energy security, 7; US-China relations, 132

enterprises: goals in Twelfth Five-Year Plan, 71. See also non-state enterprises; small and medium-sized enterprises (SMEs); state-owned enterprises (SOEs)

entrepreneurship: criminal investigations, 65; and shadow banking, 55–6; stories of, 61. See also non-state enterprises; small and medium-sized enterprises (SMEs)

environment, China: climate change mitigation, 108t, 117–18, 143–4; CO_2 emissions, 20t, 73, 85, 117, 143–4; emerging industries, 71, 86; forest degradation, 118; global governance objectives, 108t; government policies, 86–7, 118; "green city" projects, 87; public dissatisfaction, 9, 118; regulation enforcement, 9, 32; transparency, 86–7. See also energy, China

environment, US: agreements, 117–18; CO_2 emissions, 20t

equity markets. *See* financial markets, China

European Council on Foreign Relations, 48

European Union: and 2008–09 recession, 19, 21, 163n13; China's trade with, 26, 112; economic growth, 7, 19, 21, 104f; fiscal policy coordination, 21; history of transitions, 22–3

Europe Central Asia, productivity, 38f

exchange rates. *See* currency, China

exports. *See* trade

family networks. See *guanxi* networks

families: caregivers for the elderly, 36, 39–40; impact of *hukou* on, 25, 36, 39–40, 42–3; infant mortality rates, 39; one-child policy, 34, 37–8, 39–40. *See also* education; social safety net

Fan Zhai, 140–1

financial crises: Asian crisis 1997, 112–13. *See also* recession of 2008–09

financial markets, China: global governance objectives, 107–9, 108t; reforms, 56, 57–8, 60, 72, 83–4; stock markets, 52, 53, 55, 56–8, 76f. *See also* bond markets

Financial Stability Board, 107, 108t, 115

financial system, China: auditing and accounting standards, 57, 68; capital outflow, 65, 78, 157n36; disclosure of personal assets, 69; ease of doing business, 70; and economic restructuring, 26–7, 29; favoured SOEs, 53; foreign-exchange reserves (2005–12), 19, 30–2, 31t, 114; global governance objectives, 108t; goals in Twelfth Five-Year Plan, 58; government role, 54–5; impact of accession to WTO, 55, 74, 105, 109–10, 162n3; reforms proposed, 54–8, 68, 70–2, 71, 83–4; shadow banking, 55–6; sovereign wealth fund, 116. *See also* banking system; currency, China (RMB); financial markets, China; taxation

financial system, international: use of currency, 80–2. *See also* IMF (International Monetary Fund); recession of 2008–09; World Bank

Five-Year Plan. *See* Twelfth Five-Year Plan

foreign-exchange rates. *See* currency, China (RMB)

foreign-exchange reserves. *See* financial system, China

foreign investment, by China: advantages and disadvantages, 77, 84–5; affiliate companies, 78, 79, 85; agreement with Canada, 131, 165n24; capital restrictions, 56–7; failures, 111; foreign direct investment (FDI), 45, 76f, 81, 109, 130; future trends, 73, 130; global stock holdings, 76f; government role, 130; host country concerns, 78–80, 85, 111, 130; host country job creation, 130; lack of transparent governance, 130; mergers and acquisitions, 78; reciprocal market access, 130; reforms, 80, 84–5, 131, 149; sovereign wealth fund, 116–17; strategies for cooperation, 129–31; technology transfers, 111, 130–1; US investment agreements, 149

foreign policy. *See* international relations

forest degradation, 118
free trade, 104–5, 129, 138–41, 139f.
    See also FTAAP
FTAAP (Free Trade Area of the Asia
    Pacific), 110–11, 112, 129, 139–40,
    139f

"G2" bilateral relations. *See* interna-
    tional relations, China and US
G20: China's global governance ob-
    jectives, 108t; China's participation,
    4–5, 103–4, 107–9; response to
    crises, 103, 107, 109; restoration of
    IMF resources, 113
gender imbalance, 39–40
Germany: demographics, 20t, 40;
    economic growth, 17, 21–2, 22f;
    GDP comparisons, 18t; impact of
    2008-09 recession, 18t, 21; trade
    indicators, 20t
global forums: China's participation,
    4–5, 103–5, 118–19, 122, 145–6;
    participation generally, 15. *See also*
    G20; IMF (International Monetary
    Fund); trade agreements; World
    Bank
global governance, China: climate
    change mitigation, 117–18, 143–4;
    development finance, 116–17;
    financial-market oversight, 107–9,
    115–16; high-level cooperation,
    107–9; macroeconomic coopera-
    tion, 112–15; overview of objec-
    tives, 103–7, 108t, 118–19; trade
    and investment, 109–12. *See also*
    global forums; international rela-
    tions, China
global recession. *See* recession of
    2008–09
global supply chains, 74–5, 111, 139

government, China: accountability
    of, 13; and economic restructuring,
    48–9; *guanxi* networks, 12; history,
    12–13, 63; lack of checks and bal-
    ances, 28–9; and land rights, 58–60;
    municipal bonds, 42, 60; reforms
    with "Chinese characteristics,"
    12–13, 63; revenue from land sales,
    58–60; transparency *vs.* opacity,
    11–12, 13, 28–9. *See also* Commu-
    nist Party of China; corruption; Xi
    Jinping
government, US: democracy as US
    priority, 105; political polarization,
    19; US Congress paralysis, 94, 132.
    See also Obama, Barack
Green Climate Fund, 118
growth, economic. *See* economy,
    China, growth
growth-accounting framework, 8–9
Guangdong province: *hukou* reforms,
    42–3; Wukan protests, 67
guanxi networks, 12, 28, 32–3, 64

hacking. *See* cyber security
Haier, 52, 78
Hangzhou, as "green city," 87
health care: and economic restructur-
    ing, 26–7, 29, 50; health insurance,
    26, 50; *hukou* reforms, 43; private
    ownership, 72; spending on, 38,
    50
He Weifang, 66
history of China: Confucian tradition,
    12–13, 63; Mao's reforms, 12–13,
    36, 48, 63; as Middle Kingdom, 4,
    22, 24, 91, 122; three "historical
    Chinas," 23–4
Hong Kong: global stock holdings,
    76f; international financial centre,

81, 82–3; middle-income trap, 44;
trade with China, 30t
Huawei, 77–8, 111, 130
Hu Jintao: on cooperation with US
(2011), 121, 126; on corruption,
11, 27; on peaceful development,
105; on proactive planning, 107–8;
on scientific development, 13
hukou (household registration system): and education, 25, 42, 43;
and labour markets, 25, 36, 42;
land reform, 59–60; and productivity, 38; purpose, 42; reforms implemented, 42–3; reforms proposed,
8, 29, 42–3, 48; and rural families,
25, 36, 39–40, 42–3
human rights, 13, 93, 106, 128, 131,
147
Hunan province, 66
Hung Huang, 27
Huntsman, Jon, 127

IMF (International Monetary Fund):
China's objectives, 108t; China's
participation, 108–9, 112, 113,
114–15; CMIM use of IMF meth-
odology, 114; dollar-based system,
113–14; mandate, 112; response to
1997 Asian crisis, 112–13; response
to 2008 recession, 107, 113; role of
emerging economies, 104; SDRs
as reserve currency, 113–14, 115;
surveillance of members, 112, 113,
114, 115, 163n10
imports. *See* trade
income: comparison of China and
US, 32, 99; government goals, 46,
47; per capita income (2013), 24,
32, 34; projected future per capita
income, 34; and ratio of depen-

dents to workers, 34. *See also* taxation
income inequality: comparisons with
other countries, 25; and domestic
demand, 26; and economic restructuring, 26–7, 29, 46; Gini coefficient, 25; public dissatisfaction,
10, 61, 68, 131; and savings, 48; and
social programs, 9, 11; and wealth
concentration, 25–6; Xi's plan for
reform, 29
India: ASEAN+6 member, 75, 110;
BRIC dialogues, 101, 109, 147;
climate change negotiations, 117;
consumption as share of GDP,
151n5; EAS member, 137–8; income inequality, 25; relations with
China and US, 138; technology
investors, 111; trade negotiations,
141; trade with China, 30t; wealth
concentration, 26
Indonesia: middle-income trap, 44;
productivity, 38f
Industrial and Commercial Bank of
China, 19
inequalities. *See* income inequality
information technology: emerging
industries, 71; global supply
chain, 74–5. *See also* intellectual
property
"inside game": about strategies and
players, 15, 126; direct investment
flows, 129–31; domestic reforms,
131–2; expect the unexpected,
132–3; increased transparency,
127–8; meetings of top leaders,
126–9, 149; Strategic and Economic Dialogue, 128–9, 140, 142,
149; strategies to improve relations,
126–33, 149–50. *See also* interna-

tional relations, China and US; "outside game"

intellectual property: and emerging industries, 71; and legal system, 66; reforms proposed, 10, 128–9, 131; theft, 71–2; and trade initiatives, 108t, 110. *See also* cyber security

interdependence, China and US: China's holdings of US treasury bonds, 30–2, 31f; and cooperation, 6–7, 99–102, 120–1, 125; and economic growth rates, 6–7; miscalculations, 125; overview, 99–102; trade relationship, 29–32, 30t, 99–100. *See also* international relations, China and US

interest rates. *See* banking system

International Crisis Group, 89, 93, 136

International Finance Corporation, 82

international relations, China: BRIC dialogues, 101, 109, 147; China's global governance objectives, 108t; "core interests," 93, 96, 100; distrust of global systems, 104; domestic interests, 4–5, 124–5; G20 member, 107–9, 108t; high-level cooperation, 107–9; leadership expertise, 32; and North Korea, 127, 128, 132, 137, 148, 149; peaceful development strategy (2003), 95; preference for bilateral over multilateral, 119; as "responsible stakeholder," 90, 98; "soft power," 32. *See also* boundary claims; global forums; global governance, China; interdependence, China and US; international relations, China and US; military, China; trade, China

international relations, China and

US: bilateral relationship, 90–1; consensual style of Asians, 104, 112, 137, 138; cooperation framework (2011), 121, 126; cooperation *vs.* conflict, 120–4, 145–50; crisis as opportunity, 125; direct investment flows, 129–31; domestic narratives, 141–2; domestic reforms, 124–5, 131–2; economic interdependence as limit on aggression, 124; expect the unexpected, 132–3; "G2" relationship of equals, 124, 137; increased transparency, 127–8; lack of domination, 125–6; meetings of top leaders, 126–9, 149; miscalculations, 6, 88, 97–8, 99–102, 120, 125, 148; strategic distrust, 122–3; strategies to improve, 141–6; Western *vs.* Chinese values, 106–7. *See also* EAS (East Asia Summit); "inside game"; interdependence, China and US; Obama, Barack; Strategic and Economic Dialogue; trade, China; Xi Jinping

Internet: bloggers, 27; displays of income inequality, 10, 61; government websites, 27; Party dominance, 13, 62; social protests, 67; users, comparison, 20t, 32; user statistics, 10, 19, 27. *See also* cyber security

investments, foreign. *See* foreign investment, by China

Japan: APEC member, 140; ASEAN+6 member, 75, 110–11, 137–8; demographics, 20t, 23, 40; development banks, 116; EAS member, 137–8; economic growth/stagnation, 17, 21–3, 22f, 44; GDP comparisons,

18t; global stock holdings, 76f; government debt, 19; Internet users, 20t; military, 20t, 88; and recession of 2008-09, 18t, 163n13; relations with China, 105, 136, 137, 138; relations with US, 92, 122, 135, 149; TPP member, 111, 138–40; trade indicators, 20t; trade negotiations, 139f, 141; trade with China, 30, 30t, 104–5, 127. *See also* boundary claims
Jiang Zemin, 126
Jin Canrong, 103
jobs. *See* employment

Kerry, John, 100
Kindleberger, Charles, 23
Kyoto Protocol, 117–18

labour force: costs, 36–7; definition, 153n3; demographics, 35–7, 35f; growth-accounting framework, 8–9; impact of *hukou* on, 25, 36, 38, 42–3; incentive structures, 8–9; migrant workers, 36, 39–40, 42–3; minimum wage, 37; reforms, 37–8, 40, 44, 46. *See also* education; employment; rural-urban migration
Lampton, David, 90, 160n2, 161n16, 164n17, 165n22
land: corruption, 58, 67; developers and shadow banking, 56; *dipiao* (land-trading systems), 59–60; government requisition of, 29, 58, 62, 67; government revenue from, 58–60; growth-accounting framework, 8–9; and *guanxi* networks, 28; and legal system, 58, 67; property rights, 12, 28, 29, 65; reforms proposed, 10, 29, 49, 59–60, 65, 68, 70; social protests, 58, 62, 67; state monopolies, 70–1; urbanization, 58, 60
Lardy, Nicholas, 48, 151nn5–6, 152n9, 152nn11–13, 155nn1–2, 155nn6–8, 156n26
Latin America, productivity, 38f
Law of the Sea Treaty, 136
Lee Kuan Yew, 17, 123
legal system: and capital outflow, 65; comparison with Western system, 63, 106; corruption, 10–11, 64; and foreign investors, 111; and *guanxi* networks, 12, 28, 64; history of, 63; impact of WTO accession on, 162n3; judicial independence, 65, 66; land sales disputes, 58; legal education, 63, 64; Party dominance, 10–11, 63–7; reforms, 111; reforms proposed, 66–7, 68; rule of law or rule by law, 12, 63–7; and social protests, 62, 64; *weiwen* compensation for litigants, 62
Lenovo, 52, 77–8
Lieberthal, Kenneth, 122–3
Li Kequiang, 28–9, 42, 60, 147
Li Rongrong, 51
loans. *See* banking system

machinery industries, 52
Malaysia: middle-income trap, 44; productivity, 38f; trade with China, 30, 30t
manufacturing industry: emerging industries, 71; foreign investments, 78; as SOE sector, 52
Mao Zedong, 12–13, 48, 63
media coverage: and Chinese vulnerability, 5; of critics of China, 27; of cyber security, 72; of London Olympics (2012), 92, 98. *See also* Internet
Mexico and trade with China, 30t

middle class: comparison with Brazil
and S. Korea, 45; and economic
restructuring, 25–7, 29, 46; expectations of, 9, 62, 68; and international relations, 125. *See also*
consumers and consumption
middle-income trap, 6, 44–6. *See also*
economy, China, growth
military, China: boundary disputes,
88–9, 127–8; corruption, 11; cyber attacks by, 78, 85; defence
spending, 17, 19, 20t, 96–7; and
economic integration, 124; and
foreign investment, 111; increased
capacity, 4, 96–7, 123, 127–8; lack
of transparency, 96, 122–3, 127–8;
miscalculations, 125; and perceptions of US, 122; self-perceptions of
Chinese, 24, 91, 92; as SOE sector,
52; strategies proposed, 100, 122–4,
127–8, 132; as target for US's military, 127–8
military, US: Air-Sea Battle, 123;
Asia-Pacific presence, 14, 97, 123;
defence spending, 19, 20t, 96, 125;
strategies proposed, 127–8; as target for China's military, 127–8; US-
China cooperation, 132
mining and metals industries, 52–3,
78

National Development Reform Commission, 50
National Population and Family Planning Commission, 39
natural resources: foreign investment,
77; growth-accounting framework,
8–9; suppliers to China, 30. *See also*
energy, China
networks. See *guanxi* networks

"A New Type of Major-Power Relationship: Seeking a Durable
Foundation for US-China Ties"
(Lampton), 165n22
New Zealand: ASEAN+6 member,
110; EAS member, 137–8; TPP
member, 97, 138–9; trade agreement with China, 75
Nixon, Richard, 126
non-state enterprises: bonds, 57;
emerging industries, 71; foreign
investment by, 77–8; government
restrictions, 51; impact of SOEs on,
25, 78. *See also* entrepreneurship
North, Douglass, 8
North Korea, 127, 128, 132, 137, 148,
149

Obama, Barack: on cooperation with
China (2011), 121, 126; meetings
with top Chinese leaders, 126–7;
meeting with Xi (2013), 3–4, 5–6,
15–16, 147; speech to Australian
parliament, 94–5
Obama, Barack, administration: and
bilateral relationship, 100, 120
OECD, productivity (1990–2010),
38f
oil and gas, 25, 52, 143. *See also*
CNOOC; energy, China
Olympics, Beijing (2008), 101
Olympics, London (2012), 92, 98
one-child policy. *See* families
"outside game": about strategies
and players, 15, 126, 134; climate
change, 143–4; cyber security,
144–5; East Asia Summit, 97, 137–8,
139; energy security, 142–3; free
trade negotiations, 138–41, 139f;
strategies to improve relations,

141–6, 149–50. *See also* "inside game"; international relations, China and US

partnerships, China and US. *See* cooperation, China and US; interdependence, China and US
Party. *See* Communist Party of China
Patten, Chris, 34
pensions: and economic restructuring, 26–7, 29; financing of, 38; portability and labour mobility, 40; rural programs, 26, 50. *See also* retirement
perceptions, China's self-perceptions: exceptionalism, 4–5, 96, 121–2; goals of respect and dominance, 92–3; historical, 23–4, 91, 122; humiliation narrative, 14, 91–2, 98, 122; as Middle Kingdom, 4, 22, 91, 122; national pride, 4, 92–3; overview, 91–4; as poor people, 5, 24, 34; reforms with "Chinese characteristics," 12–13, 63; vulnerability, 4–5, 92
perceptions, China's view of US: as military presence, 94; miscalculations, 99–102, 125, 148; overview, 94–5, 132; strategies to improve, 141–6; as superpower in decline, 94, 101; as threat, 94, 100, 141–2
perceptions, US's self-perceptions: exceptionalism, 4, 95–6, 121–2; overview, 95–7
perceptions, US's view of China: as becoming "more like us," 12; miscalculations, 99–102, 125, 148; overview, 95–7; as protecting China's core interests, 96, 100; Romney on currency manipulation, 97–8,

99; strategies to improve, 141–6; as threat, 96, 100, 122, 141–2
Petri, Peter A., 108t, 140–1, 161nn1–2
PetroChina, 19, 52
Philippines: anti-corruption policies, 69; productivity, 38f; security alliance with US, 92; South China Sea boundary dispute, 87–9, 93, 127, 136, 138
Plummer, Michael G., 140–1
police, 62, 65–6
pollution. *See* environment
population. *See* demographics
private industry. *See* non-state enterprises
producers. *See* non-state enterprises; small and medium-sized enterprises (SMEs); state-owned enterprises (SOEs)
productivity: comparison (1990–2010), 37–8, 38f; middle-income trap, 44–6; reforms for productivity, 37–8, 40–4; reforms proposed, 47–9
property, intellectual. *See* intellectual property
property rights: and capital outflow, 65; and *guanxi* networks, 12, 28; reforms proposed, 29. *See also* land
protests. *See* social protests

Qualified Foreign Institutional Investor, 57

railways, 71, 72
real estate sector, 41, 53
recession of 2008–09: change in China/US perceptions, 94, 101; change in growth rates, 7, 17, 18t,

21; consequences, 19, 21, 115; foreign investment, 77; G20 response to, 103; IMF response to, 113, 163n13; impact on US currency, 31; US banks and international finance, 82. *See also* economy, US

Regional Comprehensive Economic Partnership, 139

registration of households. See *hukou*

renminbi. *See* currency, China (RMB)

research and development: goals in Twelfth Five-Year Plan, 40

retirement: caregiving for the elderly, 36, 39–40; raising age of, 29; and savings, 36. *See also* demographics; pensions; social safety net

Rhodium Group, 130

RMB. *See* currency, China (RMB)

Roach, Stephen, 98

Romney, Mitt, 97–8, 99

rule of law: and *guanxi*, 12; or rule by law, 12, 63–7. *See also* legal system

rural-urban migration: and economic growth, 40–1; and growth-accounting framework, 8–9; impact of *hukou* on, 25, 36; and land sales, 59; migrant workers, 36, 39–40, 42–3. *See also* agrarian society; families; urban areas

Russia: BRIC dialogues, 101, 109, 147; EAS member, 137–8; trade negotiations, 141; and wealth concentration, 25–6; WTO member, 109

SASAC (State-Owned Assets Supervision and Administration Commission), 51–2, 53–4, 79

savings: compared to investment rates, 9; and economic restructuring, 8, 26–7, 29, 42; and income inequality, 48; interest rates, 26, 29, 48, 50, 54, 55; savings rates, 9, 36, 151n7; and social programs, 26, 36, 42, 48; strategies to reduce, 26. *See also* banking system

self-perceptions. *See* perceptions

Senkaku/Diaoyu dispute. *See* boundary claims

services sector: economic restructuring, 26, 41, 72; economic slowdown, 47–8; foreign investments, 78; private ownership, 72; as SOE sector, 52

shadow banking, 51, 55–6. *See also* banking system

Shanghai: *hukou* reforms, 42; income inequality, 25; one-child policy, 39; stock market, 56–7

Shanghai Cooperation Organization, 116, 149

Shanghai Expo, 101

Shenzhen, 56–7, 71

shipping, as SOE sector, 52

Sina Weibo (blogging site), 27

Singapore: middle-income trap, 44; TPP member, 97, 138–9

Sinopec, 52, 77–8

small and medium-sized enterprises (SMEs): dividend policies, 26; and economic restructuring, 26–7; and shadow banking, 55–6

social protests: on corruption, 11, 67; Gini coefficient and potential for, 25; increase in, 61–2; land disputes, 58; repression of, 64; as traditional channel, 61–2

social safety net: and economic restructuring, 26–7, 29; financing of, 38, 42, 43; and *hukou*, 25, 42–3;

increased spending, 9, 11, 29, 50; reforms proposed, 42, 43, 48, 60, 70; SOE dividends to finance, 38, 43, 51, 54. *See also* families; income inequality

SOEs. *See* state-owned enterprises (SOEs)

solar energy, 53, 86, 118

South Africa, 25, 117

South China Sea boundary dispute. *See* boundary claims

South Korea: APEC member, 140; ASEAN+3 member, 75, 110; EAS member, 137–8; economic reforms, 45, 46; middle-income trap, 44; security alliance with US, 92; TPP potential member, 139–40, 139f; trade with China, 30, 30t, 104–5

sovereign wealth funds, 113, 116

spying. *See* cyber security

State Council, 68

State Environmental Protection Administration, 86

state-owned enterprises (SOEs): capital outflows, 78; corporate bonds, 57; corruption, 11; dividend policies, 26, 38, 43, 51, 54, 70; and economic restructuring, 26–7, 29, 52–4; foreign investment by, 77–80, 84–5; goals, 52–3, 77; goals in Twelfth Five-Year Plan, 71; government role, 51, 52–4, 78–9; host country concerns, 78–80; number of SOEs, 52; oversight by SASAC, 51–2, 53–4, 79; Party domination, 13, 24, 54; as per cent of GDP, 155n11; profitability, 51, 52; reforms proposed, 29, 43, 52–4, 70, 71–2; sectors preferred, 51–2, 53, 71, 78; stock markets, 52; subsi-

dies, 24, 25, 50–1; "zombie" firms, 53

steel industry, as SOE sector, 52–3

stock markets. *See* financial markets, China

Strategic and Economic Dialogue (S&ED), 93, 128–9, 140, 142, 149

Suzhou, as "green city," 87

Taiwan: and China's core interests, 92, 93, 96; middle-income trap, 44; trade with China, 30, 30t; and US-China relations, 94, 126, 128, 137

taxation: of capital gains, 70; and economic restructuring, 26–7, 29; and government's role, 49–50; of income, 48, 50; of property, 60; reforms proposed, 49–50, 70

technology industries: emerging industries, 71; global supply chain, 74–5; as SOE sector, 52; technology transfers, 111, 129–30. *See also* intellectual property

telecommunications industry, 52, 72, 78, 79, 130

Thailand: middle-income trap, 44; productivity, 38f; TPP potential member, 139–40, 139f

Tibet: and China's core interests, 93, 131; US reception of Dalai Lama, 94

TPP (Trans-Pacific Partnership): China as non-member, 97, 100, 111–12, 129, 139, 140, 141; economic benefits, 140; mandate, 97; members, 97, 138–9; trade negotiations, 139–41, 139f; trade standards, 100, 110–11, 140; US influence, 97, 110–11, 129, 138–9, 140, 141

trade: comparative indicators, 20t; and currencies generally, 80–2;

free ridership of small economies, 106–7; investor protection, 111; negotiation templates, 139–41; tariff barriers, 140; value of total goods, 153n19. *See also* interdependence; WTO (World Trade Organization)

trade, China: and boundary disputes, 88–9; with Canada, 131, 165n24; and capital outflow, 65, 157n36; China's holdings of US treasury bonds (2001–13), 31f; and domestic demand increase, 26; ease of doing business, 70; and economic restructuring, 26–7; exchange-rate flexibility, 26, 57, 113; foreign-exchange reserves, 19, 30–2, 31t, 114; global governance objectives, 108t; global supply chains, 74–5, 111; global trade, 29–32, 75f; import/export statistics (2011), 29–30, 30t; middle-income trap and stagnation, 6, 44–6; miscalculations, 97–8; reforms proposed, 70–1; savings/investment rates and trade surplus, 9; US-China free trade, 129, 141, 146, 149; US trade deficit, 74. *See also* currency, China; trade agreements, China; WTO (World Trade Organization)

trade, US: APEC member, 140; comparative indicators, 20t; and cyber security, 144–5; global stock holdings, 76f; global trade, 75f; TPP member, 138–9, 140, 141; trade with China, 29–32, 30t, 74; US-China free trade, 129, 141, 146, 149. *See also* interdependence; recession of 2008–09; TPP (Trans-Pacific Partnership)

trade agreements: APEC negotiations, 110, 140; ASEAN agreements, 136, 138–40, 139f; bilateral agreements, 75, 149; bilateral US-China trade, 146; China's ambivalence, 104–6; free trade, 104–5, 129, 138–41, 139f; negotiation tracks, 139–40, 139f; regional agreements, 75–6, 138–9, 149; US influence, 141. *See also* ASEAN (Association of Southeast Asian Nations); FTAAP (Free Trade Area of the Asia Pacific); TPP (Trans-Pacific Partnership)

Trans-Pacific Partnership. *See* TPP (Trans-Pacific Partnership)

Twelfth Five-Year Plan: education, 40; emerging industries, 71; environment strategy, 87, 118; exchange-rate reforms, 115; financial targets, 58; renewable energy, 160n21; research and development, 40

UN Conference on Trade and Development (UNCTAD), 76

UN Convention on the Law of the Sea, 89

unemployment. *See* employment

UN Framework on Climate Change, 108t, 143

United States: energy, 27, 130, 132; environmental issues, 20t, 117–18. *See also* cooperation, China and US; currency, US; economy, US; government, US; interdependence, China and US; international relations, China and US; military, US; Obama, Barack; trade, US; and entries beginning with *perceptions*

urban areas: demographics, 40–1, 41f; employment, 41; land development, 58, 60; one-child policy, 39;

reforms, 7, 38, 41; social benefits, 50; social protests, 62. *See also* rural-urban migration
urbanization and productivity, 7, 40–2, 41f. *See also* economy, China, growth

vehicle ownership, 19, 20t
Vietnam: productivity, 38f; South China Sea boundary dispute, 87–9, 93, 136

Wang Jisi, 122–3, 124–5
Wang Quishan, 28, 69
weiwen compensation for litigants, 62
Wen Jiabao: disclosure of personal assets, 69; on economic growth, 47; on economic sustainability, 8
Wenzhou, Zhejiang, 55–6, 71
wind power, 86, 118. *See also* environment
World Bank: China's participation, 108t, 116–17; index of ease of doing business, 70; response to 2008 recession, 107; role of emerging economies, 104; study on reforms *(China 2030)*, 28–9, 47, 70
WTO (World Trade Organization): China's accession to, 55, 74, 105, 109–10, 162n3; China's domestic reforms, 55, 105, 109; China's participation, 108t, 109–10; dispute resolution, 109–10; response to

2008 recession, 107; trade and investment, 109–10
Wu Bangguo, 63
Wukan protests, 67

Xi Jinping: on boundary disputes, 89; on "Chinese dream," 13; on cooperation with US, 100, 121; on corruption, 11, 27–8, 68–9; disclosure of personal assets, 69; domestic priorities, 147–8; meetings with top US leaders, 126–7; meeting with Obama (2013), 3–4, 5–6, 15–16, 147; on power relations, 6; as provincial governor, 12; reforms proposed, 29; southern tour of China by, 29; strategies to improve US-China relations, 142. *See also* Communist Party of China; government, China
Xinjiang region as core interest, 93, 131

Yang Jiechi, 93, 120
Ye Shiwen, 92
Yu Keping, 66

Zhang Gaoli, 129
Zhejiang province: shadow banking, 55–6
Zhou Qiang, 65–6
Zhou Xiaochuan, 113
ZTE foreign investment, 130